VISUAL GUIDE · ANTONI GAUDÍ COLLECTION · BARCELONA

The Basilica of the

Sagrada Familia

A TEMPLE CONVERTED INTO A UNIVERSAL WORK OF ART

PHOTOGRAPHS: CARLOS GIORDANO RODRÍGUEZ AND NICOLÁS PALMISANO SOSA

DOSDEARTE EDICIONES   GUÍAS VISUALES GRANDES OBRAS

CONTENTS

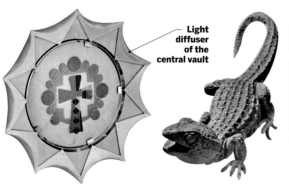

Light diffuser of the central vault

↩ **Nature as a model**
Antoni Gaudí was inspired by living beings as much for the development of functional solutions as for the aesthetic and decorative purposes of the basilica.

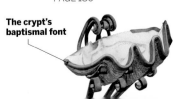

The crypt's
baptismal font

01 | A WORK FOR THE PEOPLE
The origins of Antoni Gaudí's basilica

The construction of the Temple of the Sagrada Familia started in 1882 on a site in Barcelona's new Eixample.

The nineteenth century was a complicated period for Christianity in Europe, and Barcelona, a city that was undergoing great social and economic change during this period, was a paradigm of these difficulties. The Church, which had wielded great influence throughout the entire history of Spain, saw its authority greatly challenged due to the action of the successive liberal governments that held power in the decades following the French Revolution and the War of Independence. The ecclesiastical confiscations dictated in 1836, whereby the State expropriated lands and assets that the Church had accumulated over the centuries, plunged the institution into a deep economic crisis. Moreover, a section of Spanish society had to undergo a radical change in habits brought about by the Industrial Revolution and by the consequent shift from eminently rural customs to a new urban lifestyle. This process brought with it a spiritual crisis that the Spanish clergy combatted with the fevered missionary activity of numerous ecclesiastics of the time, determined to recuperate the lost faith of millions of citizens. The foundation in 1866 of the Association of Devotees of Saint Joseph was part of this reaction by the Church to recover its spiritual influence on society. The fact that by 1878 the association already had half a million members encouraged its creator, bookseller and philanthropist Josep Maria Bocabella, to take up the construction of an expiatory temple dedicated to the Holy Family, subsidised by worshippers' donations on a plot of land in the Eixample, the new district drawn up in the city after the demolition of the medieval walls. After several years of preparation, building work started on the 19th of March, 1882.

⦿
The Nativity façade
The state of the building work on the eastern façade of the temple in the period 1906-1907, with the structure already quite advanced.

⦿
The Adoration of the Shepherds
A close-up of one of the sculptural groups that are found on the Charity portico, on the Nativity side.

19th century Barcelona

The construction project of Sagrada Familia falls within the context of a period of great social, economic and cultural vitality in the City of Barcelona.

A new cultural order

During the 19th century, Barcelona underwent a rapid process of industrialization that turned it into a rich and active city. This vigour moved into the world of culture with the dawn of the *Renaixença* (Rebirth), a movement devised to give the Catalan language back the cultural status it had acquired during the Middle Ages and which led to great progress in literature, art and architecture. In this process, championed by a new and thriving middle-class that had made its fortune from industrial production, the recognition of the Catholic faith as the foundation of Catalan medieval splendour played an important role and was also the basis for the new capitalist morality of the *Renaixença*: a renewed, moderate and conservative nationalism with Christian roots which believed the spirit of the Catalan nation resided in family, property and religion.

The centre of the new Barcelona
Plaza de Cataluña, was, already by the late 19th century, the vital core of a rapidly expanding city.

1881

IS THE YEAR
the Virgin of Montserrat, a romanesque sculpture known as *La Moreneta*, (small, dark lady) is made Patron Saint of Catalonia.

1875

ALFONSO XII, KING OF SPAIN
The Bourbon dynasty recuperates the throne after the failure of the reign of Amadeus I and the 1st Spanish Republic.

1885

THE FIRST AUTOMOBILE
The German engineers Daimler and Benz manufacture the first combustion engine.

1898

INDEPENDENCE OF CUBA
After the war against the USA, Spain loses control over the island, which achieves independence.

1905

THEORY OF RELATIVITY
German scientist Albert Einstein revolutionises the foundations of physics with his formula E=mc2.

The Eixample project
The grid layout of the new Barcelonan neighbourhood surrounds the old city centre.

1,500
HECTARES
equivalent to a similar number of football fields, is the surface area of the Eixample devised by town-planner Ildefons Cerdà.

Town planner Ildefons Cerdà
Born in 1815 and died in 1876, he was behind the creation of the Eixample project of the City of Barcelona.

Medieval wall
The overcrowded conditions in which Barcelonans lived led to the wall's demolishment in the year 1854.

The Eixample of Barcelona
The growth of the city in the 19th century can't be understood without the demolition of the walls in 1854 and the later development of the surrounding plain with the Eixample plan. This was devised by town-planner Ildefons Cerdà, who created a grid of perpendicular and parallel streets made up of blocks with chamfered corners. In 1881, Bocabella acquired one of these blocks in order to build the Sagrada Familia on it.

1912
THE 'TITANIC' SINKS IN THE ATLANTIC
The world's largest transatlantic liner goes down on its first voyage after hitting an iceberg.

1918
END OF THE GREAT WAR
German surrender puts an end to the First World War, where nearly ten million people perished.

1926
TELEVISION ARRIVES
The Scottish engineer John Logie Baird was the first to person to send moving pictures.

The temple's developer

The creation of the Basilica of the Sagrada Familia is due to the initiative of a bookseller, publisher and Barcelonan philanthropist, Josep Maria Bocabella i Verdaguer, founder of the Association of Devotees of Saint Joseph.

El Propagador
It was the official publication of the Association of Devotees of Saint Joseph, where the intention to build a temple was first expressed.

Veneration for Saint Joseph

A cultured and devout Catholic, Josep Maria Bocabella was owner of an old bookshop, *Herederos de la Viuda Pla*, which printed books since the 17th century, many of religious theme. Fuelled by a deep adoration for Saint Joseph, he founded in 1866 the Association of Devotees of Saint Joseph, with the aim of encouraging Christian family values. Four years later, he travelled to Rome to present Pope Pius IX with a silver image of the Sagrada Familia. On his return, he passed through the Italian town of Loreto, which is where the dwelling is conserved in which, as the story goes, lived Jesus, Mary and Joseph in Nazareth. Amazed by the symbolic and artistic fundaments of this sanctuary, the visit inspired him to construct a replica in Barcelona of the Holy House, an initiative that would end up turning into the start of the Basilica of the Sagrada Familia.

The author of the work
Josep Maria Bocabella (Barcelona, 1815-1892), passed away when only the crypt area had been concluded.

Josep Maria Bocabella
He was a great advocator of the figure of Saint Joseph.

1892
IS THE YEAR
in which Josep Maria Bocabella died, buried in the Sagrada Familia crypt.

Papal coat of arms
The pontiff's symbol presides over the post that commemorates the laying of the basilica's first stone.

The Nativity façade
It narrates the early years of Jesus' life.

THE LORETO SANCTUARY. BOCABELLA'S INSPIRATION

Located in the Italian town of Loreto, the sanctuary holds the Holy House, the place where the archangel Gabriel told Mary she would be a mother and where the Holy Family resided. In the 13th century the house was supposedly transferred from Nazareth to where it is at present.

House of the Holy Family

Interior of Loreto's temple

The first stone
The ceremony of the laying of the basilica's
first stone, which all civil and ecclesiastical
authorities of the city attended.

The first architect

014

Josep Maria Bocabella commissioned the construction project of the Expiatory temple of Sagrada Familia to Francisco de Paula del Villar, the diocesan architect, who had offered his services free of charge.

Del Villar's neo-Gothic project

Bocabella had the idea to construct an exact replica of the sanctuary in Loreto which was home to the Holy House, but Del Villar convinced him not to do so but to build instead a neo-Gothic temple, in accordance with the historicist trends prevailing at the time. The project, inspired by great medieval cathedrals, foresaw the building of a church with three naves, with Latin cross ground plan, a crypt of notable size, an apse with seven chapels and a bell tower with spire that, located over the portico, would have reached 85 metres high, half the height of the largest tower in Gaudí's later project. This verticality, joined by the design of exterior buttresses and large honeycombed windows, gave the building a clear Gothic identity. The first stone was laid on the 19th of March, Saint Joseph's day, in 1882, which was followed by the construction of the crypt.

Francisco del Villar
Born in Murcia in 1828 and died in Barcelona in the year 1901, Del Villar was Sagrada Familia's first architect.

Neo-Gothic project
Francesc del Villar's design proposed a main façade that included a wide staircase as well as five entrance ways.

1882

IS THE YEAR
when the Sagrada Familia's first stone is laid, months after the purchase of the plot of land within the Eixample.

DEL VILLAR. HIS MAIN WORK

Built between 1876 and 1884, the Neo-Romanesque apse on the monastery of Montserrat is the main work of Del Villar, who counted on Gaudí as draftsman.

Del Villar's original project
The architect's first solution was a Gothic-Romanesque style hybrid and it was crowned by a large central cimborio.

Access from Mallorca Street

Buttresses

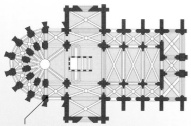

Ground plan. With 3 naves, transept and apse.

1

The bell tower
The culminating point of Del Villar's project was going to be eighty-five metres tall and located over the entrance way.

2

Cimborio of square ground plan

The apse
It incorporated seven chapels placed in semi-circular fashion, as in the definitive project, but it was lower in height than the one designed later on by Antoni Gaudí.

Work on the basilica in 1882. The first part undertaken was the crypt.

Del Villar's sketches
The temple's first architect tried, at least, three constructive solutions.

1885
IS THE YEAR
in which the first mass in the crypt of Sagrada Familia is held.

Del Villar's withdrawal
In 1883, just a year after the start of the building work, Del Villar resigned from managing the project due to differences with Bocabella and his main consultant, the historicist architect Joan Martorell. Del Villar defended the erection of crypt pillars based on solid stone ashlars, while Martorell and the temple's developer, more concerned about the cost of the project, believed that covering them with stone and filling the inside with cement was sufficient. Finally, Bocabella accepted the resignation of Del Villar for fear of going bust.

Rose window of medieval inspiration

Side entrance on eastern side

Joan Martorell
Technical architect to Bocabella, Gaudí's teacher, who then recommended him to lead the project.

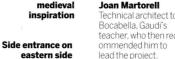

The crypt's pillars. The discrepancies with the developer over his construction method were the reason for architect Del Villar's resignation.

Gaudí takes on the project

Following Del Villar's resignation, Bocabella offered the management of the building work to Joan Martorell, his consultant, but the latter declined and recommended his most talented disciple: an architect aged 31 called Gaudí.

Chair designed for Casa Calvet
As well as his architectural abilities, Gaudí stood out for his sensitivity in industrial design and the decorative arts and in his projects he took charge of devising the furniture and the decoration.

The work of a lifetime

In 1883, when he accepted Bocabella's commission, Gaudí was directing his first two complete works: Casa Vicens, in Gràcia (Barcelona), and the Caprice, in Comillas (Cantabria). Despite having only five years experience, the architect enthusiastically took up the challenge that would mark his entire career up until his death, in reply to the trust that Martorell, his mentor, had placed in him. Initially, Gaudí contemplated changing the the temple's orientation in order to construct it diagonally on the site, to gain more building surface area, directing the entire Nativity façade towards dawn and the Passion façade towards dusk. However, the advanced progress of the work on the crypt, with the foundations finished and the columns started, obliged him to keep the orientation decided by Del Villar.

43
YEARS
were dedicated by Gaudí to managing work on the Sagrada Familia, twelve of them exclusively.

Rosette from Ciutadella Park

Gaudí's workshop
With the passing of the years, Gaudí became so involved in the work on Sagrada Familia that he moved into his workshop in the year 1925.

Casa Vicens (Barcelona)

The Caprice (Comillas)

Casa Batlló (Barcelona)

Park Güell (Barcelona)

> **ANTONI GAUDÍ**
>
> The temple is the construction *par excellence* and, after that, only the house"

← **Gaudí settles in Barcelona**
In 1868, at the age of 16, he moves to the Catalan capital in order to start his secondary education.

1878
IS THE YEAR
Gaudí qualifies as architect, in whose graduation, the School's director said "I don't know if we've given the degree to a madman or genius".

Güell Palace
It was architect Antoni Gaudí's first major project for his patron, industrialist Eusebi Güell.

31
YEARS OF AGE
was Gaudí when he started directing the work on the Expiatory temple of the Sagrada Familia.

Casa Milà
Known as La Pedrera, this building on Passeig de Gràcia is one of Gaudí's most important works.

90
PROJECTS
were carried out by Gaudí throughout his career amongst finished works, various collaborations and unfinished projects.

A GENIUS' CAREER
Antoni Gaudí's life

An obsessive dedication to his architectonic vocation and the premature loss of many of his loved ones mark the almost seventy-four years of life of Gaudí.

1852
He was born on the 25th of June in Reus, though some claim he was born in Riudoms.

1873
He starts his architecture studies.

1876
He collaborates with Josep Fontserè on Ciutadella. His brother and mother die.

1878
He graduates as architect. He designs Casa Vicens. He meets Eusebi Güell, his great friend and patron.

1882
He is Joan Martorell's assistant.

1883
He takes on Sagrada Familia. He starts the Caprice and Casa Vicens.

1884
He plans the lodges of Finca Güell.

1890
He finishes Güell Palace.

1900
He finishes building work on Casa Calvet. He starts Park Güell.

1904
He starts the refurbishment of Casa Batlló.

1905
He plans Casa Milà, known as La Pedrera.

1906
He moves into Park Güell with his father who dies a few weeks later as well as his niece Rosa Egea.

1911
Ill with Maltese fever he moves to Puigcerdà.

1914
Construction work on Park Güell grinds to a halt. He dedicates himself solely to Sagrada Familia.

1918
His friend and patron Eusebi Güell dies.

1925
He moves into his workshop in Sagrada Familia.

1926
The seventh of June he is run down by a tram. He dies three days later and is buried in the crypt of the Temple of Sagrada Familia.

The temple's evolution with Gaudí

The architect took charge of the construction project of the Sagrada Familia in the year 1883 and was its director for forty-three years, up until his death in 1926. Just a few weeks after taking on the post he had already totally changed the project, not only its aesthetic and structural appearance, but in the magnitude and significance of the work. After introducing subtle but relevant changes in the crypt –started before his arrival– Gaudí shows off all his creative genius on the apse, the cloister and the Nativity façade, his great architectonic legacy, and leaves his successors a detailed constructive plan that includes solutions full of ingenuity and originality for the naves and the towers that have to top the arrangement.

02 | IN SEARCH OF THE PERFECT TEMPLE
Gaudí's project

The Basilica of the Sagrada Familia is testimony to Antoni Gaudí's artistic evolution over four decades.

Gaudí took charge of the building work in 1883 and combined the temple's construction with his other projects, until the year 1914 when he decided not to take on any more commissions and to dedicate himself exclusively –up to his death in the year 1926– to the Basilica of the Sagrada Familia. These forty-three years enabled the architect to understand that his project was able to achieve what for centuries other architects before him had not managed: to construct a perfect temple. With this objective, he ploughed all his effort into providing the basilica arrangement with all the necessary elements in order that they would be in perfect consonance with its final mission: the celebration of Christian liturgy. Accordingly, Sagrada Familia reflects all the stages of Gaudí's artistic, architectonic and symbolic growth. With the passing of the years and propelled by his crav-

ing for perfection, the architect became more and more knowledgeable about religion whilst his faith grew even stronger. In this respect, he converted into an expert on liturgical themes, which is evident throughout the temple, devising Sagrada Familia as if it were a large stone bible where the history and mysteries of the Christian faith are told. In this regard, the exterior of the basilica represents the Church, by means of the Apostles, the Evangelists, the Virgin and the Saints; the cross that tops the main tower symbolises the triumph of Jesus' church; the façades relate the three key moments in Christ's life –his birth, death and resurrection and glory–; the interior refers to the universal Church and the crossing, to Celestial Jerusalem. Antoni Gaudí managed to combine his faith and his artistic genius to transform the Sagrada Familia into a universal masterpiece.

Passion façade
Facing the west, this side of the temple symbolises the pathway of Jesus Christ up to his crucifixion and death.

Wrought iron cover
Attributed to Antoni Gaudí, its function was to cover a hole located alongside the temple.

Undulated organic forms

The work of a lifetime

After several decades of intense study of architectonic structures and Christian liturgy, Antoni Gaudí left his successors the project of the perfect temple, an ideal place for prayer and religious worship.

⊖
Decoration of the apse's stone
Representations of the zone's fauna and the secular world, the reptiles used to decorate the apse walls are related to evil.

Criteria of proportionality

Gaudí set out to erect a building of enormous dimensions on a Latin cross ground plan with five naves, a crossing, an apse, an exterior cloister style ambulatory, twelve bell towers, six cimborios and three façades: the Nativity and the Passion, on either side of the transept, and the Glory, at the start of the naves. As in other works, the architect devised the project with proportional criteria. Taking a module base of 7.5 metres, he designed the interior measurements of the temple to follow a close mathematical relationship. For example, he planned the interior to be ninety metres long (twice the module), sixty metres wide (two-thirds of the length) on the crossing and forty-five metres wide (half the length) on the naves.

The Nativity
It symbolises the legacy of the Son of God and is located on the Charity portico.

The crypt
Below the temple's presbytery, it adopts the semi-circular shape of the apse.

✳
Basilica of the Sagrada Familia

1
The Glory façade

2
Jesus' tower or cimborio

3
Bell towers
There are 12 (four each façade) and they symbolise the apostles.

7
DOORS
are on the Glory façade, each one of them dedicated to a sacrament.

Monument to fire
Gaudí planned a monumental torch with several arms.

Staircase
It overcomes the difference in levels.

The Passion façade

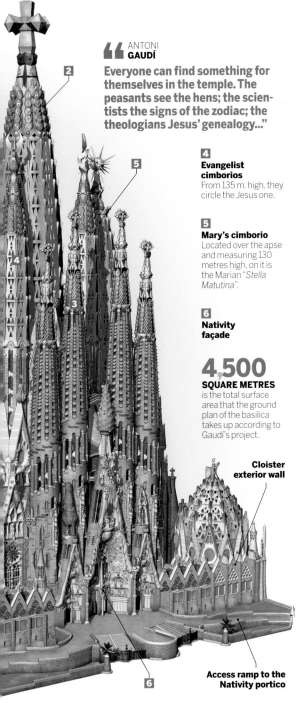

ANTONI GAUDÍ

> Everyone can find something for themselves in the temple. The peasants see the hens; the scientists the signs of the zodiac; the theologians Jesus' genealogy..."

4 Evangelist cimborios
From 135 m. high, they circle the Jesus one.

5 Mary's cimborio
Located over the apse and measuring 130 metres high, on it is the Marian "*Stella Matutina*".

6 Nativity façade

4,500 SQUARE METRES
is the total surface area that the ground plan of the basilica takes up according to Gaudí's project.

Cloister exterior wall

Access ramp to the Nativity portico

Central nave. Gaudí devised the inside of the temple like a forest.

Interior staircase of the towers

The vault over the crossing

A tie between heaven and earth

Gaudí sought to make Sagrada Familia a link between heaven and earth, recuperating the hunger for verticality that medieval cathedrals had pursued. He wanted to erect the highest building in Barcelona and devised Jesus' cimborio –an element topping the basilica at 172.5 metres high– to tower over all other civil constructions in the city, whilst at the same time preventing a work carried out by Man from exceeding a work created by God, and for this reason he kept it lower than Barcelona's mountain, Montjuïc.

The temple's preliminary studies

Antoni Gaudí's original work method, based on the concept of an initial generic project that would adapt accordingly to construction progress, resulted most appropriate for a project as vast as the Sagrada Familia.

Parabolic tower

2

Upper floor

1

Constantly changing projects

Gaudí devised projects as continuous evolutions parting from a generic idea, subject to last minute changes. It is not surprising then, that with the Sagrada Familia, a commission to which he dedicated more than four decades, this process of constant change would prove very intense. Moreover, because he was working simultaneously on other commissions the architect could experiment with certain structures on a smaller scale and later apply them to the temple. Such is the case of the Franciscan Missions of Tangiers –a project signed in 1892 for the construction of a church, a hospital and a school in Morocco, which were never built– and, above all, the unfinished church of the Güell Colony, where Gaudí used models for the first time to simulate the layout of self-supporting structures without having to carry out calculations.

⊖ Güell Colony crypt
Gaudí experimented with new methods that he later applied on the basilica project, such as hyperbolic, paraboloid shaped surfaces or funicular structures.

Tangiers Mission project
The shape of the towers was a source of inspiration for the Sagrada Familia.

1898

IS THE YEAR
when Gaudí starts the project of the construction of a church in the Güell Colony.

DRAWINGS. THE ORIGINAL PROJECT

Gaudí used to do drawings and sketches to record the profiles that sprung from his imagination. This study of the arrangement of the temple, drawn in 1902, reproduces an elevation of the building seen from the western side, with the façade of The Glory seen in perspective.

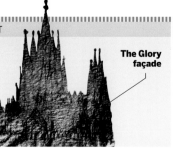

The Glory façade

⊖ Town development plan around temple
Gaudí planned the surroundings of the basilica like a star-shaped square in order that, from four angles, all of the Sagrada Familia could be seen, including the tower that was dedicated to Jesus.

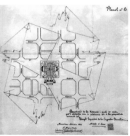

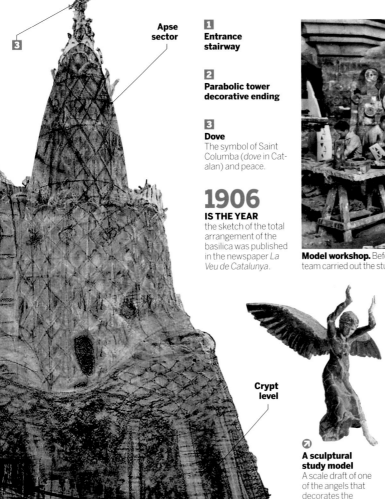

Apse sector

1 **Entrance stairway**

2 **Parabolic tower decorative ending**

3 **Dove**
The symbol of Saint Columba (*dove* in Catalan) and peace.

1906
IS THE YEAR
the sketch of the total arrangement of the basilica was published in the newspaper *La Veu de Catalunya*.

Crypt level

Model workshop. Before the construction of any part of the temple, Gaudí's team carried out the studio models to scale.

⌷ A sculptural study model
A scale draft of one of the angels that decorates the Nativity façade.

The model as a base
After outlining the general plan of the project, Gaudí transferred the different elements of the temple to the blueprint, resolving the structural challenges that arose by using large models on the scale of 1:10 and 1:25. In 1936, ten years after his death, the wave of anticlerical attacks that followed the start of the Spanish Civil War provoked a fire in his workshop and practically all the plans and drawings were lost. The models, in contrast, were restored and used to continue the work in accordance with Gaudí's ideas.

➔ Photographic studies
In order that the sculptures' gestures could be as realistic as possible, Gaudí used people, dolls and even skeletons as models, which he had photos taken of to serve as inspiration for the sculptors.

Study skeleton

Model for a figure of Christ

Figure carried out in wire

A revolutionary structure

The spiritual forest Gaudí devised within the temple to provide worshippers with an atmosphere for prayer and retreat represents the technical and artistic peak of the architect's career.

The reinvention of the Gothic style

Using the great medieval cathedrals as inspiration, Gaudí proposed for Sagrada Familia the reinterpretation of the Gothic style as a necessary concept in order to establish a close relationship between heaven and earth by means of height and light. To achieve this, large windows had to be included which subsequently meant that walls could not be load-bearing. This was how the architect came up –after many years of study– with the solution of tree-like columns, an avant-garde system that had never been used up to that time, where loads could be transferred down to the floor by means of the branching out of columns.

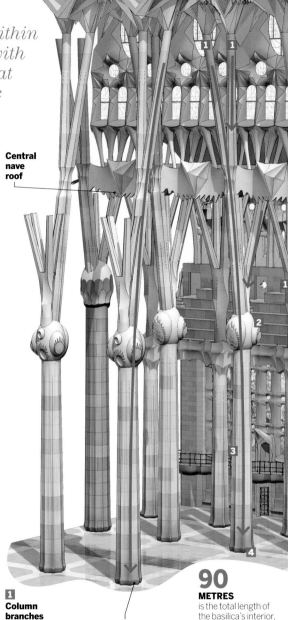

Central nave roof

The nave structure
The columns of the central nave tilt as they increase in height in order that they are able to withstand the weight coming from the vaults.

A forest
The inspiration for the design of the vaults and columns of the central and lateral naves can be found in trees.

60
METRES
is the height that the vault of the crossing reaches, the highest one out of those on the naves' ceiling.

Funicular model of the Güell Colony
This revolutionary and intuitive method facilitated the deduction of the structure of the basilica's naves.

1 Column branches
They withstand the vault weight.

Column with eight-sided base

90
METRES
is the total length of the basilica's interior, between the Glory façade and the apse.

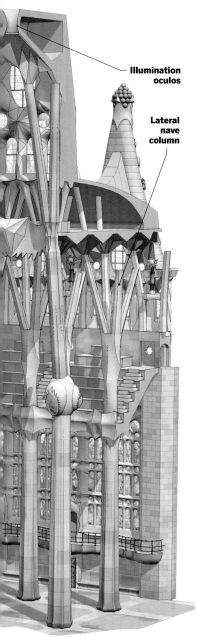

Illumination oculos

Lateral nave column

3
Column shaft
It is the column's main element, between the capital and the base.

4
Column base
It transfers the loads to the foundations.

➡ **The central nave**
Supported by two rows of arborescent columns, the central sector of the inside of the temple reaches a height of forty-five metres.

2
The nodes
They absorb the central and lateral naves' loads and are inspired by the natural transition between a tree trunk and branches.

The funicular model

Gothic structures enabled building to a great height, but cathedral walls required robust buttresses to absorb the loads coming from the roof. In order to avoid reinforcements that were deemed unsightly, Gaudí devised an innovative system: first of all he created a model using ropes; after, he tightened them by hanging small weights from them; consequence of the resulting tensions, the ropes took on the shapes of archways, called funiculars, which the architect then interpreted as the shapes that would enable self-supporting structures to be built; lastly, he took a photograph of the model and then turned the image around in order to obtain the structure.

THE THREE SOLUTIONS. EVOLUTION OF THE STRUCTURE OF THE NAVES

Neo-Gothic solution

Parabolic solution

Hyperbolic solution

Gigantic dimensions

Despite being limited to the moderate dimensions of a block in the Eixample, the temple designed by Gaudí reaches extraordinary magnitudes, especially in height.

THE LENGTH OF A JUMBO JET
The Boeing 747, one of the largest aeroplanes, would look tiny next to the towers.

70.66 metres

6
CIMBORIOS
Four of them are dedicated to the Evangelists, one to Jesus and another, situated over the apse, to the Virgin.

12
BELL TOWERS
symbolise the twelve Apostles and culminate the three façades of the Sagrada Familia.

Passion façade towers

172.5
METRES
is the height of Jesus' cimborio, culminating point of the entire arrangement.

Football field
The total length of the Sagrada Familia is equivalent to a football pitch.

110 metres

28
GIRAFFES
put one on top of the other would reach the height of the cimborio dedicated to Jesus.

The Apostle bell towers

Tree of life

Nativity façade

COMPARISON. THE HEIGHT OF OTHER TEMPLES

69 M

Nôtre Dame Cathedral

137 M

Saint Peter's in the Vatican

157 M

Cologne Cathedral

COMPARATIVE SURFACE AREAS

Saint Peter's Cathedral of London	27,000 m²
Seville Cathedral	23,400 m²
Saint Peter's Basilica in the Vatican	23,000 m²
Milan Cathedral	12,000 m²
Hagia Sophia in Istanbul	10,000 m²
Cologne Cathedral	7,000 m²
Nôtre Dame in Paris	4,800 m²
Basilica of the Sagrada Familia	**4,500 m²**

135
METRES
is the height of the Evangelists' cimborios, which are five metres higher than the Virgin Mary's.

130
METRES
is the height that the Virgin Mary tower measures, which is topped by a twelve-pointed star

14,000
PEOPLE
is the maximum number of worshippers that are allowed inside the Sagrada Familia, including the chorus.

1 Evangelist cimborios

2 Decorative roof endings

Glory façade

Monument to fire

3 Jesus' cimborio

2

4

3

Virgin Mary cimborio

Apse vault

4 Transept on Nativity side

Apse

THE DEPTHS OF THE BASILICA

03 | The crypt

Gaudí rapidly left his mark on the construction of the crypt, where he combined symbology and functionality.

The crypt, a word whose Greek origin means *hidden*, is an underground space commonplace in medieval churches. Its source goes back to the mausoleums that were excavated in rocky zones where martyrs were laid to rest during the early years of Christianity, in order to protect remains from desecration in a period in which the Christian faith was clandestine. Centuries on, when these martyrs were canonized, it became common practice to build a temple over the crypt where the body was kept, so that they could be venerated and their memory properly honoured. From this ancient practice arose the layout typical of crypts in Romanesque and Gothic churches: they are vaulted spaces that are much lower than the temples covering them and they are supported by thick pillars which are capable of withstanding the weight of the building that towers above. Normally located below the church's high altar, crypts often reproduce the profile of the presbytery and lack natural light due to the fact that they are underground. Equipped with this historical and architectonic knowledge, Gaudí assumes the task of the Sagrada Familia and immediately leaves his own particular stamp on the construction of the crypt, started the year before by his predecessor Francesc del Villar. Although he took on the project set on maintaining the former neo-Gothic style, he was capable of converting this space –traditionally dark, enclosed and with low ceilings– into a spacious area that was brighter and better ventilated. These modifications radically changed the arrangement and made it apt for worship where, since 1930, it has been used as Sagrada Familia's parish. It was designated a World Heritage site in the year 2005.

The ambulatory
Of semi-circular shape, the corridor that separates the chapels from the central area of the crypt is covered by eleven Gothic cross vaults.

Symbology
Antoni Gaudí used quite a large variety of materials for the decoration of the crypt, following a strict symbolic program.

Gaudí's first decisions

The architect put all his architectonic ingenuity into play in order to improve the area of the crypt without having to redo the ground plan of the arrangement nor change the layout of the columns that his predecessor had planned.

Illumination
Gaudí designed most of the lights in the crypt, such as those decorating the chapels that surround the altar.

1
Winding access staircases

The crypt's structure

The excavation of the crypt started on the 19th of March 1882 –coinciding with the celebration of Saint Joseph's Day–, under architect Francisco del Villar's management, who resigned just a few months into the building project. His place was taken by –now 1883– the young Gaudí, who initially planned on bringing in significant changes to structure and arrangement of space but who, for economic and budgetary questions, decided not to carry them out and ended up maintaining the existing structure started by his predecessor. Thus, the layout of the crypt: seven apsidal chapels –one of them dedicated to Saint Joseph– in semicircle shape, an ambulatory, a spacious central area and another five chapels where the central altar is located.

Stained glass
The opening of a trench round the crypt led to the installation of stained glass in the neo-Gothic windows.

11
COLUMNS
that are joined to each other are on each of the pillars that support the crypt's vaults.

The baptismal water font
The bowl is a shell from the Philippines , resting on a wrought iron structure.

The basilica high altar

2

6

7

3

The structure
The apsidal chapels are distinguished between the thick pillars that support the crypt's structure.

2
Gaudí's tomb
The remains of the architect rest in the Chapel of Our Lady of Mount Carmel, to the left of the altar.

3
Chapel of Saint Joachim and Saint Anne

Chapel of Saint John the Evangelist

1891

IS THE YEAR
when the crypt structure was covered and completed, which had taken nearly ten years of construction work.

9

METRES
is the depth reached under the temple's chevet in order to house the crypt structure.

5
The ribs on the vaults
The entire roof of the crypt is formed and supported by simple and compound cross vaults.

Apsidal columns

1

6
The central altar. It is located below the basilica's high altar.

5

4

Chapel of the Immaculate Conception

Exterior retaining wall

The Sacred Heart chapel's windows

4
Saint Joseph chapel
Presided by the saint's image, it occupies the central apse and it was the first one to be finished in 1885.

7
Sacristy door
It is decorated with curved and straight metal ornaments.

2

METRES
is the height the crypt exceeds in relation to the level of the temple.

Gaudí's contributions

The architect introduced several changes to the crypt planned by Del Villar. Structurally, he had a trench built around the underground level in order to improve ventilation and illumination. With the same purpose, he raised the vault of the central area of the crypt and installed windows that overlook the inside of the church, under the high altar, and absorb the natural light from the naves. His contributions, however, were not just structural, given that he topped pillars with capitals carved with patterns taken from nature.

CHRONOLOGY. THE CRYPT'S PHASES OF CONSTRUCTION

1882
The crypt's start
After the laying of the first stone excavation work begins.

1885
Work advances
The first masses are celebrated at Saint Joseph's altar.

1936
The Civil War
During the conflict the crypt underwent serious damage.

The twelve chapels

The crypt holds twelve chapels: seven of them follow the profile of the apse and are dedicated to advocations related to Jesus' family; the other five are located on the front wall, one of which incorporates the high altar.

Capitals with plant motifs
One of Gaudí's first interventions in the temple was the redesign of the capitals with themes taken from nature.

Dedicated to the Holy Family

The crypt's chapels are organised into two groups. On one side, the apse chapels, dedicated to saints related to the Holy Family and other advocations, are dedicated to Saint Elisabeth and Saint Zachariah –the Virgin's cousins–, the Immaculate Conception, Saint Joseph – the Holy Family's patriarch and patron of the association founded by the temple's developer–, the Sacred Heart of Jesus, Saint Joachim and Saint Anne – the Virgin's parents– and Saint John the Baptist, son of Elisabeth and Zachariah, and Saint John the Evangelist. On the other side, Gaudí arranged, on the opposite wall, the five other chapels, one of which is also the central altar and is presided over by a modernist carving of the Holy Family. The oratories at the far ends are dedicated to Our Lady of Carmel and to the Holy Christ, and hold the remains of Gaudí and Bocabella.

Frame work of Gaudí

Work of sculptor Josep Llimona

The relief of the Holy Family
Josep Llimona's altarpiece on the high altar was originally in Casa Batlló's chapel.

Saint Joseph's Chapel
Sketch by Gaudí of how the chapel should be.

1892
IS THE YEAR
in which Josep Maria Bocabella dies and is buried in the crypt.

Chapel of the Holy Christ

Saint Joseph's Chapel

Chapel of the Sacred Heart

Chapel of Our Lady of Carmel

The crypt paving
Work of Italian artist Mario Maragliano, the mosaic that covers the crypt floor is an allegory of the sacrament of the Eucharist.

The symbolic decoration

The extraordinary artistic personality of Gaudí is apparent in the crypt thanks to the ornamental details carried out in carved stone, polychrome, mosaic work, wrought iron, glass and numerous other materials.

Craftwork

Shackled by the structural plan of the decisions of his predecessor, Gaudí concentrated in particular on the decorative and symbolic aspects in order to give the crypt its own identity. Firstly, he substituted the Corinthian endings planned for the capitals with plant motifs, in accordance with his naturalistic conception of architecture. Once the crypt's structure was concluded, he designed the symbolic program of the chapels with the supervision of Bocabella and the aid of numerous artists and craftsmen close to him. That is to say, Gaudí had winged angels sculpted –to be used as column pedestals–, he proposed the mosaic theme that decorates the paving of the central area and designed the sacristy door and the keystones that decorate the vaults, as well as the stained glass windows and the lamps that illuminate the chapels.

◆ The winged angels
The seven apsidal chapels are decorated with angels inspired by the Apocalypse of Saint John.

Painted stone

Seven-winged angel

28
ANGELS
with two, four and six wings adorn the corbels of the columns of the apsidal chapels of the crypt.

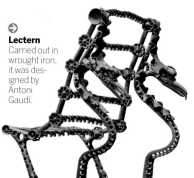

◆ Lectern
Carried out in wrought iron, it was designed by Antoni Gaudí.

The Holy Family

The Chapel of Jesus Christ

The Chapel of Montserrat

Naturalistic decoration
Throughout the crypt, Gaudí devised a decorative scheme full of plant motifs such as flowers, branches and leaves.

1

Stained glass windows
The windows are executed with naturalistic, colourful motifs.

2

The Chapel of Montserrat
Fresco on the chapel's wall referring to the sacred mountain.

Halo
The aureole is gold polychrome.

3

Decorated walls
Polychrome reliefs and bas-reliefs are employed to decorate the crypt walls.

Wings wrap around an angel

Saint Joseph's Chapel
Mosaic, part of the phrase "*Ora pro nobis*" on either side of saint.

40×30
METRES
are the interior dimensions of the crypt's semi-circular ground plan, located below the temple's altar.

Polychrome
In the Saint Joseph Chapel there is the only angel that Gaudí coloured in the style of the sculptures of Gothic cathedrals.

1

2

3

Mosaic of The Chapel of Jesus Christ

THE CHAPEL OF CARMEL. GAUDÍ'S RESTING PLACE

Located on the far left-hand side of the front wall of the crypt and presided over by a carving of the Virgin, the chapel of Our Lady of Mount Carmel holds architect Antoni Gaudí's tomb, who lies, just as he expressed when alive, under a restrained tombstone of black stone.

Pedestal

Our Lady of Carmel

The cross vaults

The complete roof of the crypt, modified by Antoni Gaudí in order to improve the original project, is a combination of artistic ingenuity and beauty over a classic structure of cross vaults that are typical of the Gothic style.

A brighter crypt
The relief of the central sector of the crypt means the space can make the most of greater natural illumination.

Withstanding the temple's weight
For its underground location and below the tremendous weight of the apse walls, the crypt of the Basilica of the Sagrada Familia stays up thanks to two concentric rows of large pillars of oval section, which form ogival archways and support the weight of a total of 22 Gothic style ribbed cross vaults. Ten of them cover the chapels of the arrangement, another eleven make up the ambulatory and the largest covers the centre of the crypt with a complex radial solution based on twelve ribs that stem from a large keystone decorated with a scene from the Annunciation, work of sculptor Joan Flotats. This central vault goes two metres above the ceilings surrounding it. This difference, meant the architect could put openings high up in the arches, overlooking the basilica's interior to provide more light and ventilation.

Central vault. Gaudí designed it to be higher than the rest.

22
KEYSTONES
with polychrome work top the vaults of the Temple of the Sagrada Familia's crypt.

Close-up
Carved stone decoration is at the end of the ribs of the vaults.

Keystone relief of the central vault
Depicting Mary's Annunciation, sculpted and polychromed by Joan Flotats.

Vault keystones

Ambulatory keystone

Saint John the Baptist's Chapel

Saint Joseph's Chapel

The Immaculate Chapel

The angels in the decoration of the crypt. In the symbolic program planned by Gaudí and Bocabella for the subterranean space of the temple the angels take on a special relevance, which appear carved in stone as corbels in the chapels, as reliefs on the keystones of the ambulatory and also in stained glass windows that overlook the exterior ditch. In all cases, these two, four and six-winged or trumpet-carrying angels refer to the narration of the Final Judgement that Saint John the Evangelist relates in the Book of the Apocalypse.

04 | The apse

THE PERFECTING OF THE GOTHIC STYLE

Gaudí dedicated the apse façade to the consecration of the Virgin Mary, to whom he was particularly devoted.

The Christian faith of Antoni Gaudí grew in an exponential way during the forty-three years he was at the helm of the building work on the Sagrada Familia, due to a constant feedback between the temple and its creator. Actually, from a very early age he had already professed a fervent devotion to the Virgin Mary, built up throughout his childhood and youth in his native city –Reus–, whose patron saint is the Madonna of Mercy. In fact, the worship of Mary experienced an age of splendour in the second half of the 19th century, in particular dating from 1854, when Pope Pius IX proclaimed the Dogma of the Immaculate Conception. Imbued by this existing devotion to the Virgin in Europe and by his own Marian convictions, Gaudí decided to dedicate the entire arrangement of constructions on the apse's façade –Mary's tower, the apse and the Assumption Chapel–

to Jesus' mother and, as a counterpoint, he dedicated the seven interior chapels of the temple's chevet to the Sorrows and Joys of Saint Joseph by express wish of Josep Maria Bocabella, developer of the work. In this way Antoni Gaudí –well read on the history of ecclesiastical architecture and Christian symbolism– provides each one of the façades of the Basilica of the Sagrada Familia with a defined significance, with the apse being chosen to hold the greater number of Marian elements. Precisely for this reason and continuing with this allegorical coherence, the architect decides to locate one of the six cimborios planned for the temple on the apse side: a monumental tower reaching 130 metres high with a sculpture that represents the *Stella Matutina* or the Morning Star, an ancient Marian image that symbolises the dawn and dusk of each day.

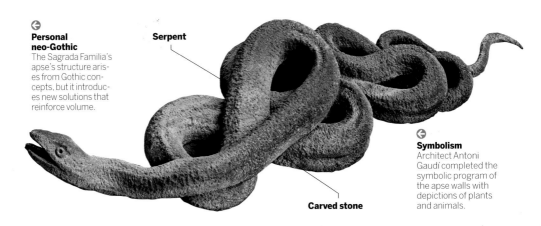

Personal neo-Gothic
The Sagrada Familia's apse's structure arises from Gothic concepts, but it introduces new solutions that reinforce volume.

Serpent

Carved stone

Symbolism
Architect Antoni Gaudí completed the symbolic program of the apse walls with depictions of plants and animals.

A renewal of the Gothic

With the construction of the apse, Gaudí reformulates the neo-Gothic style of his predecessor with a different approach orientated towards naturalism, where animals and plants invade the area.

A traditional structure

Legacy of the *absidia* that rounded off ancient Roman basilicas, the presence of the apse as the chevet's protective wall has characterised churches since the early days of Christianity. As was the tradition in the majority of artistic styles throughout history, Sagrada Familia's apse has a semi-circular ground plan, a shape that helps focus the worshippers' attention on the altar, found in the centre of the chevet (a Gothic church's far-east end). In fact, by taking on the crypt's neo-Gothic structure, Gaudí accepted the same layout for the apse, given that the latter is no more than the projection of the crypt towards the temple's upper levels. And, as in the case of the crypt, this structure generates seven chapels within the basilica.

Founding saints
Their images can be found in the niches of the apse.

Gothic forms
Gaudí used shapes from the Gothic period, such as pinnacles.

1

2

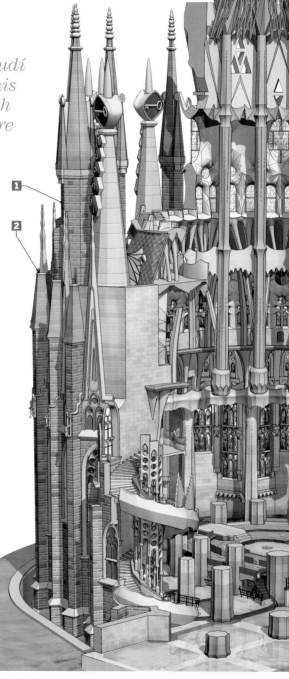

||||||||||||||||||||||||||||||||||||||||||||||||

CHRONOLOGY. THREE YEARS OF CONSTRUCTION

1891
Building starts
The underground structure serves as a base for the apse.

1892
The wall
The semi-circular shape that makes up the apse is built.

1893
The pinnacles
Narrow endings culminate the sector's construction.

Pinnacle

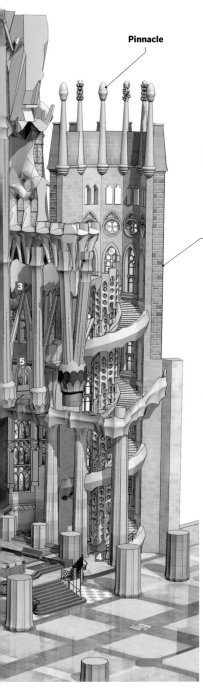

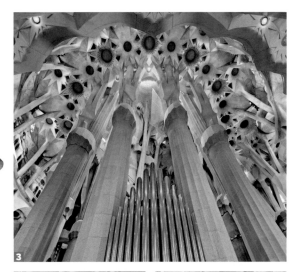

20,000
SCREWS
were required to put up the scaffolding used on the construction of the apse.

Snail
Its presence indicates the location of the winding staircase.

50
METRES
is the height that the apse's pinnacles reach.

2
Plant details
They top the arrises and the pinnacles that crown the wall.

3
Apse vaults
They follow the nave scheme, with skylights giving zenithal light.

4
Ambulatory
It separates the chapels from the high altar.

5
Upper part of apse
It holds the choir stalls designated for the use of child choirs.

Gaudí's first elevation of the apse
The Gothic style's verticality prevails in the initial design of the temple's northwest sector.

A personal style
The apse structure responds to Gaudí's creative genius, whose "perfecting of the Gothic" describes the designs he introduced in this section. As well as persevering to support walls without resorting to buttresses, the architect also exaggerated arrises so chiaroscuros would be created to underline the apse's volume. Likewise, he topped the apse with pinnacles that highlighted verticality, reinforced the splendour of the cimborio, and the apse was decorated with depictions of flora and fauna that show his love of nature.

Nature in stone

The ogival windows and the apse's pinnacles are of Gothic inspiration, but whereas medieval sculptors created imaginary beings, Gaudí refers to his mentor, Mother Nature, and reproduces animals and plant forms in his work.

Saint Clare of Assisi
Amongst the sculptures of the founding saints of religious orders is the founder –at the start of the year 1200– of *The Order of Poor Ladies*.

Realist fauna

With a symbolic and decorative proposal that was quite daring for the religious customs prevalent in the late 19th century, the architect had numerous sculptures of reptiles, amphibians and species from far off lands put into place on the exterior walls of the apse, creatures which at the time were deemed to be of lower rank, in order to carry out a triple function: decorative, their large size made them easily visible from the street; functional, for their use, such as the gargoyles, to drain rainwater from the temple roofs; and symbolic, given that they were beings associated with evil since ancient times that, positioned head down, flee from the mystic power of the symbols that top the towers representing Jesus and Mary –the cross and *Stella Matutina*– and they seem to wander around the façade, with no possibility of entering the temple.

The gargoyles
Gaudí used common animals traditionally related to evil.

Lizard

The claws are highly realistic

8
FOUNDING SAINTS
preside over the apse, amongst which stand out Saint Francis of Assisi and Saint Teresa of Jesus.

1893
IS THE YEAR
in which the construction work on the semicircular wall that defines the outside of the apse is finished.

Snail

Sea snail

Frog, symbol of evil

Chameleon, inconstancy

1
Rainwater drainage

2
Ear of wheat
Gaudí chose this cereal as a eucharist symbol, the base of the bread that Jesus gave his disciples.

3
Wild herbs
The architect chose to depict some species of Mediterranean plants that were found on the temple's site.

50
CENTIMETRES
is the size of the grains of the ears of wheat that act as decoration for the apse.

SYMBOLIC UNIVERSE
The anagrams
The stylised pediments of the apse culminate in pinnacles that contain the anagrams of Jesus Christ, the Virgin Mary and Saint Joseph, the Holy Family.

Anagram of Jesus Christ. It is accompanied by the Greek letters *alpha* and *omega*, which mean the start and end.

Dynamic, moving sculptures
Gaudí represented the animals escaping from the basilica's divine influence.

➡ **Anagram of Jesus**
The initial of the name of the Son of God is surrounded by a crown of thorns, symbol of his calvary.

⬅ **Joseph anagram**
The initial 'J' is represented surrounded by daffodils, flowers that evoke the purity and chastity of the saint.

➡ **Virgin Mary anagram**
The crown located over the initial 'M' for Mary symbolizes her condition as Queen of Heaven and Earth.

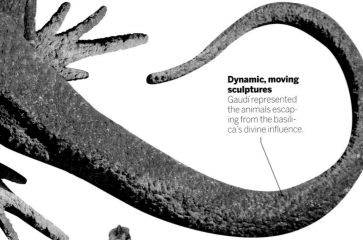

✳ Wild herbs

1.80 m

Plants with Christian symbolism
In contrast to the allusions to the animal kingdom in the wall decoration, the pinnacles that finish off the apse are topped with sculptural representations of plant species connected to the Christian faith, such as ears of wheat –symbols of the Eucharist–, the palm leaves, the olive, the cypress, the cedar tree or lavender.

The interior of the apse

Just as in the crypt, the semi-circular structure of the apse, divided outwardly into nine apsidioles, results in seven chapels in the interior as well as two stairwells, situated at the far ends.

The Holy Family
The central chapel holds a copy –the original is found in the crypt– of the altarpiece carved by Josep Llimona which depicts Saint Joseph, the Virgin Mary and Jesus.

The apsidal chapels

Continuing with the symbolic coherence of the basilica, Gaudí dedicated the apsidal chapels to the seven sorrows and joys of Saint Joseph and provided them with separate spaces –of pentagonal structure– facing the ambulatory, in a free interpretation of medieval Gothic cathedrals where height, illumination and sound were three fundamental concepts. In that sense he planned the chapels in such a way to receive light from two places: on one side from the large, Gothic style windows –designed to be filled with different coloured stained glass– and, on the other, from higher up by means of the lanterns. The third concept, sound, he also decided to introduce it into the apse, locating over the seven chapels –and throughout the length of the apse's entire perimeter– the continuation of the choir gallery of the nave used for the child choir.

350
CHILDREN
can sing in the choir gallery that is built over the apse's chapels.

Tabernacle
The tabernacle with the phrase "I am the life", situated in the apse's central chapel.

The ambulatory
A spacious area to pass through separates the oratories from the high altar.

ANGELS. SYMBOLISM

Finding inspiration in the decorative and symbolic solutions of Gaudí for the crypt chapels, sculptor Jaume Cases depicts the Apocalypse of Saint John with the stone angels that decorate the columns' corbels of the apse chapels.

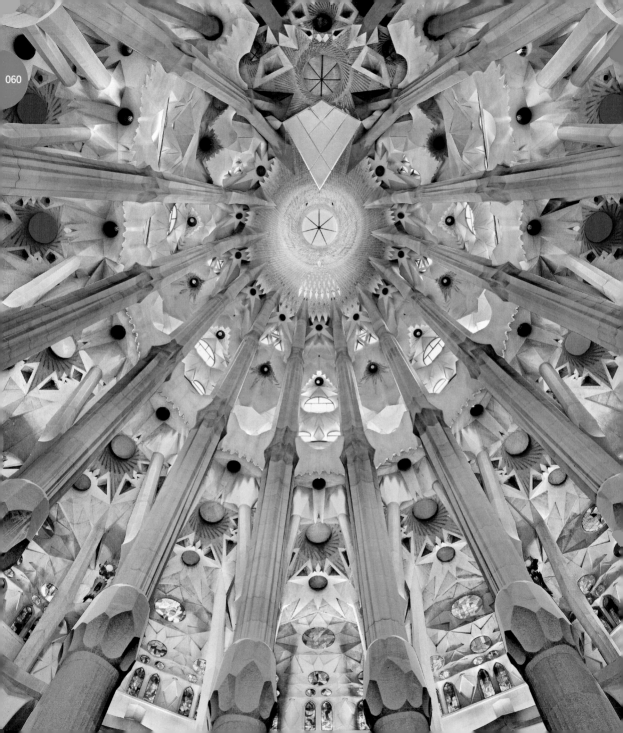

The upper structure of the chevet. Marked by the semi-circular ground plan of the apse, the chevet vertically develops in three stretches, from below to above: the apsidal chapels illuminated by high Gothic windows, decorated with stained glass of abstract theme; the stand with terraces reserved for the choirstands for the children's choir, culminated by seven lanterns, one over each chapel; and, highest up, the enormous structure of Mary's tower, which will top the arrangement of the apse with a cimborio measuring 130 metres high.

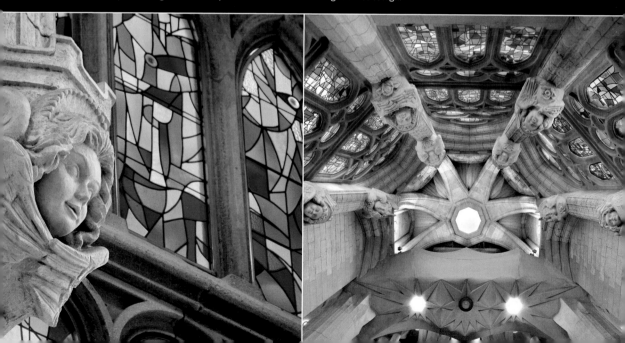

05 | THE PERIMETER THAT ISOLATES THE BASILICA
The cloister

Gaudí designs an original and innovative cloister in response to the spacial limitations of the plot of land.

Fundamental elements of medieval religious architecture, cloisters came about in monasteries as an evolution of atriums in Roman dwellings and of the first palaeo-Christian basilicas. All the rooms in monasteries were connected and organised around this quadrangular arcaded and generally landscaped courtyard. During the Middle Ages and up to the late nineteenth century, the period in which construction on the Sagrada Familia commenced, the cloister was a basic element not only for monasteries, but for cathedrals and for the majority of large churches that had to provide rooms for canons or religious orders. It was always put to one side of the church, parallel to the naves, with which it was connected via a highly ornate portal. However, in the first project of the Sagrada Familia, Francisco del Villar did not foresee the construction of a cloister.

In contrast, Antoni Gaudí, whose apprenticeship had been strongly influenced by Historicism that extolled the recuperation of medieval styles, took on the work whilst searching for a means to include a cloister in the project. With the crypt already started and located right in the centre of the block meant the traditional layout of an arcaded courtyard would prove to be impossible. Gaudí, however, demonstrated great practicality and proposed a revolutionary solution, never seen before in the history of religious architecture: a cloister that went right around the temple, cutting it off from the hustle and bustle of the surrounding streets and allowing the basilica to be able to enjoy the peaceful and tranquil atmosphere typical of a monastery. With this solution, moreover, the architect recuperated the true significance of the cloister, which is to enclose.

The cloister's windows
The first design of the pediment of the walls proposes three triangular windows with three circular openings in each one.

The Rosary portal
On the cloister's entrance –to the north of the Nativity façade–, Gaudí arranged a decoration of carved stone roses.

An innovative cloister

Gaudí revolutionises the concept of the cloister in order to add new utilities to its traditional purpose: to reduce the noise that came from the street and to allow the holding of processions down its arcaded corridors.

Gaudí's solution

Antoni Gaudí designed the cloister of the Sagrada Familia as an arcaded, rectangular passageway whose four sides correspond to the four façades. It is formed by the repetition of multiple stretches or modules of rectangular ground plan, roofs with cross vaults and topped with triangular pediments. Despite being an enclosed space, and despite the absence of a garden –an element that is put in the centre of many traditionally shaped cloisters– the natural illumination of the arcaded corridor designed by Gaudí is assured thanks to the windows and rose windows that overlook the exterior in each one of the modules. Likewise, as the level of the ground is at the same height as the naves of the temple, the architect takes advantage of the difference in height with the street in order to create a mezzanine that can be used for different purposes.

Sculptural finish. Close-up of an overflow.

⊙ Wall termination
Located on top of the pediment, it is carved in stone and has geometric shapes.

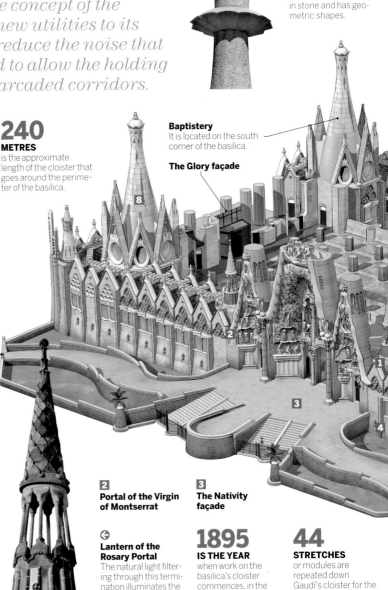

240 METRES
is the approximate length of the cloister that goes around the perimeter of the basilica.

Baptistery
It is located on the south corner of the basilica.

The Glory façade

② Portal of the Virgin of Montserrat

③ The Nativity façade

⊙ Lantern of the Rosary Portal
The natural light filtering through this termination illuminates the portal's detailed sculptural decoration.

1895 IS THE YEAR
when work on the basilica's cloister commences, in the zone that surrounds the Nativity façade.

44 STRETCHES
or modules are repeated down Gaudí's cloister for the Basilica of the Sagrada Familia.

4 First solution for the walls

Cross vault

5 Second solution for the walls

Parabolic vault

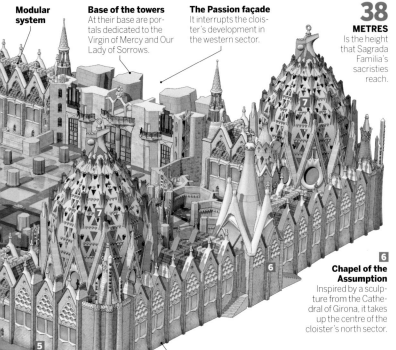

Modular system

Base of the towers
At their base are portals dedicated to the Virgin of Mercy and Our Lady of Sorrows.

The Passion façade
It interrupts the cloister's development in the western sector.

The apse façade

5

7

6

38 METRES
Is the height that Sagrada Familia's sacristies reach.

The cloister's portals and buildings
Gaudí plans a series of architectonic solutions to provide continuity to the cloister's perimeter. He designs two entrances on the Nativity dedicated to the Rosary and Montserrat Virgins, and two more on the Passion dedicated to Mercy and Sorrows. He also devises four buildings on the corners –two sacristies, the baptistery and the Chapel of Penance– and the Chapel of the Assumption in the centre of the apse's façade.

6 **Chapel of the Assumption**
Inspired by a sculpture from the Cathedral of Girona, it takes up the centre of the cloister's north sector.

Angels on the Rosary Portal

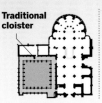
The sacristies
Put on the cloister's north and west corners, they have a squared base measuring 18 metres and a 12 paraboloid cupola.

7

8 **The Chapel of Penance**
It takes up the cloister's east corner, next to the Glory façade.

INNOVATION. A NEW CONCEPT OF CLOISTER

While traditional cloisters are put to one side of the church, Gaudí's cloister wraps around the entire temple, separating it from the hubbub of the street.

Traditional cloister

Gaudí's cloister

Symbology and decoration

Gaudí combines functional aspects with allegorical ones, in an avant-garde cloister devised as a space which divides Sagrada Familia's interior –the spiritual side– from its exterior –the earthly side–.

The Virgin Mary's sign
On the keystone of the archway on one of the stretches of cloister is the classic anagram of the Virgin: her name's initial topped by the ducal crown.

Between the spiritual and earthly

When devising the cloister like a barrier that isolates the basilica, Antoni Gaudí imagined this space as a frontier between the secular –the exterior– and the spiritual –the interior–, a symbolism that he would use years later in the Park Güell project. In this symbolic framework, the Sagrada Familia's cloister represents the earthly world, which the architect conceived as a space for the holding of processions and decorated its doors with roses –symbol of the rosary and, in traditional cloisters, of the heavenly–, and with olive branches and palm leaves, which recall Jesus' entrance into Jerusalem. In order to be able to complete the symbolism planned, the architect puts into place, on the cloister's exterior walls, anagrams of the *Sagrada Familia* or Holy Family, helicoidal columns and elements alluding to nature.

The Holy Family
Anagram formed by Jesus' cross, Joseph's carpenter's saw and the Virgin Mary's initial.

Bouquet of roses
Vault keystone of the cloister of the Montserrat Portal.

1899
IS THE YEAR
in which the Rosary Portal is finished, to the north of the Nativity façade.

EVOLUTION. SOLUTIONS FOR THE PEDIMENTS

1890
THE FIRST SOLUTION
Gaudí plans the pediments based on three ogival modules inspired by Gothic art.

1919
THE SECOND SOLUTION
The architect updates the initial proposal with a layout that is rather like honeycomb.

✱ Vault keystone
An angel dancing whilst holding the rosary in its hands is depicted on the keystone on the portal dedicated to the Virgin of the Rosary.

The Rosary portal

With the aim to connect and provide continuity to the cloister, Gaudí plans a doorway, on each intersection with the Nativity and Passion façades, where four dedications to the Virgin Mary stand out.

Virgin of the Rosary
The central sculpture of the tympanum represents the Marian dedication to which the entire portal is dedicated to, with Jesus in her arms.

An example for the future

Antoni Gaudí knew he wouldn't be the architect to complete the four portals of the façades and thought he had better leave a finished model behind so those who continued on with his work would have a prototype they could refer to and follow. With this idea he dedicates the only portico that he got to finish to the Rosary Virgin, in which he designed a complex and detailed arch with two archivolts decorated with sculptures of characters from the Old Testament, illuminated zenithally by a conically shaped lantern. On this same line, he arranged the sculptures of the Rosary Virgin and Saints Domingo and Catalina on the portal's tympanum. Despite his efforts to leave his legacy behind, the original sculptures on this portal were destroyed in 1936 with the anticlerical assaults that occurred during the first days of the Civil War.

1983
IS THE YEAR
in which Japanese sculptor Etsuro Sotoo, residing in Barcelona, finishes the portal's restoration.

The stained glass
On the wall's upper zone, the circular shapes of the windows are decorated with stained glass.

The structure of the portal
Three tri-lobulated arches frame the tympanum presided over by the Rosary Virgin.

Isaac, Abraham's son

Jacob, Isaac's son

Solomon, King of Israel

David, King of Israel

* **The Temptation of Man**
It symbolises violence: the devil offers a worker an Orsini bomb, used by anarchists at the start of the 20th century.

1

The fish-like devil

The Temptation of Woman

The Death of Just

Cupola of the lantern over the portal

➔ **The bomb that went off in the Liceo**
The explosion of an Orsini bomb in Barcelona's Liceo Theatre in 1893 inspired the sculpture of 'The Temptation of Man' on the Rosary Portal.

Le Petit Journal
SUPPLÉMENT ILLUSTRÉ

1

Roses sculpted out of stone

In honour of the Rosary Virgin, all the constructive elements that make up the portal –such as the walls, the vaults and the arches– are decorated with roses carved from stone, one of the most commonly used symbols to represent the Virgin Mary in general and to the dedication of the Rosary in particular.

The sacristies

On the north and west corners of the basilica and on either side of the apse, Gaudí put two large sacristies that connect with the cloister and whose outer shape reminds of baptisteries from the Renaissance.

Two buildings with six floors

Sacristies are rooms in churches that are used to store objects necessary for liturgical celebrations. These rooms are usually found inside the church, but Gaudí decided to make the most of the original layout of the cloister in order to put them on the corners, alongside the apse. Similar to the baptisteries of the Italian Renaissance, they have a squared base, which is internally divided into six levels or floors, connected by a winding staircase. Outside, each sacristy is divided into two parts: a stone wall that reproduces the structure of the stretches of the cloister and, supported over this base, a cupola carried out by means of 12 paraboloids perforated with triangular openings to ensure illumination.

Ground plan drawn by Gaudí
The architect engraved in stone his study of the sacristy.

12
SIDES
make up the sacristy cupolas, inscribed within an 18 by 18 metre square base.

Definitive solution for the sacristies
Gaudí carried out the sacristies' ground plan in 1923.

1
Ground floor
With a surface area of 350 square metres, the main floor of the sacristies directly connects to the cloister.

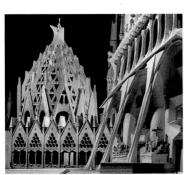

A model of one of the sacristies

Attached section of the staircase
It is separate from the sacristy and has a winding staircase.

Grape vine
The symbol of Jesus' blood decorates the cupola.

2
Floors of the sacristy
The columns that support the interior structure of the Sagrada Família tilt towards the centre.

8
METRES
is the height of the main floor of the sacristies that Gaudí designed for the Sagrada Família.

Illumination hollows

3
The obelisks
They top the corners of the cloister, symbolising the cardinal points.

4
Upper level of the sacristy

6
LEVELS
are within, all perfectly illuminated thanks to the numerous openings.

5
Exterior decoration
The cupola is covered with stone, brick, ceramic decoration and *trencadís*.

Three-dimensional development
Study of the construction of the sacristy cupola.

SCULPTURAL ARCHITECTURE
Chapel of Assumption of the Virgin

Gaudí designs a small temple of vertical proportions and puts it in the centre of the cloister's northern stretch, near the apse.

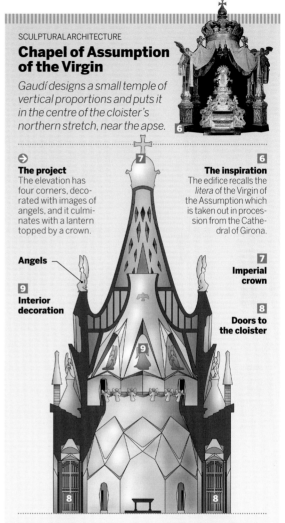

The project
The elevation has four corners, decorated with images of angels, and it culminates with a lantern topped by a crown.

6
The inspiration
The edifice recalls the *litera* of the Virgin of the Assumption which is taken out in procession from the Cathedral of Girona.

Angels

9
Interior decoration

7
Imperial crown

8
Doors to the cloister

Sketch of the façade

Initial study of the chapel

30
METRES
is the height reached by the lantern that provides natural light to the Assumption Chapel, topped with an imperial crown, the symbol that usually finishes off the images of the Virgin Mary.

06

A SPACE DEVOTED TO WORSHIP
A SPACE DEVOTED TO WORSHIP

The basilica interior

Gaudí plans a conservative ground plan and reserves innovations for the temple's vertical projection.

In Ancient Greece, the *agora* or main meeting point incorporated a *stoa basiliké*, a large space where justice was carried out, divided into three naves by two rows of columns. This building was used by the Romans for the same purpose and with a similar layout: it was an edifice of rectangular ground plan, with three or five naves –the central one with the highest ceiling– and a raised gallery from which judges presided over trials. From the fourteenth century, with the Emperor Constantine's conversion to Christianity, basilicas transformed into places of worship for the new religion, with these columned structures of ancient civic tradition used as models for churches. This progressive Christianisation of basilicas led to a key change in this type of building: the adoption of the cross ground plan, a shape that symbolises the presence of Christ in the temple and which is

defined with the addition of a nave –also known as transept– that transversely crosses the basilica. The passing of the centuries and artistic styles did not change this layout, to the point that, in 1883, when taking charge of the management of Sagrada Familia, Gaudí found himself with a project that suggested the construction of an interior with Latin cross ground plan, a scheme in which the transept is found closer to the head of the church. Sensible yet daring at the same time, Antoni Gaudí kept the drawing of the ground plan –which he only retouched in order to increase it to five naves– and ploughed all his creative genius into the search for a revolutionary solution for the vertical projection of the temple, marked by an avant-garde structure that does away with buttresses due to the invention of arborescent columns and hyperbolic vaults.

The central nave
The slightly tilted arborescent columns mark the path up to the high altar, the focus of attention in the celebration of religious ceremonies.

The custodias
Gaudí designed 24 custodias –Christian liturgical objects used to place the blessed sacrament– to put over the choirstands.

A mystic forest

The numerous columns that make up the interior of the basilica create a unique atmosphere that lends itself to contemplation, prayer and spirituality.

An atmosphere for prayer

Gaudí wanted to convert the inside of the Basilica of the Sagrada Familia into a large forest in which the structure of columns, vaults and roofs would work by imitating trees, with the trunk, the branches and, covering the structure, the foliage which the sun light filters through. This innovative solution was designed to create a transcendental atmosphere appropriate for prayer and meditation and to provoke a contrast with the ground plan, in which the architect opted for a traditional structure of five naves, divided up by four rows of columns and crosscut by a transept, and a presbytery where the high altar is found –significantly raised above the level of the rest of the temple–, an ambulatory and seven radial chapels.

Gaudí's studies
The architect spent more than three decades on different versions of the naves.

Computer assisted development
Technology has helped make the basilica's interior reality.

4,500
SQUARE METRES
is the total surface area of the interior spaces of the Sagrada Familia.

The high altar
The altar from which the basilica's religious ceremonies are carried out is below the apse's vault.

Liturgical furniture
Gaudí designed confession boxes and other objects to be used for the purpose of worship.

Main entrance
It is carried out via the Glory façade.

Tree-shaped columns
Gaudí devised a new type of column that divided into several branches starting from the nodes.

45
METRES
is the maximum height of the vaults that cover the central nave.

Pinnacles of the windows

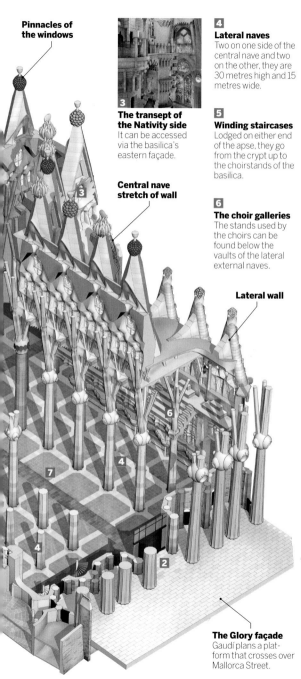

The transept of the Nativity side
It can be accessed via the basilica's eastern façade.

Central nave stretch of wall

Lateral wall

4 Lateral naves
Two on one side of the central nave and two on the other, they are 30 metres high and 15 metres wide.

5 Winding staircases
Lodged on either end of the apse, they go from the crypt up to the choirstands of the basilica.

6 The choir galleries
The stands used by the choirs can be found below the vaults of the lateral external naves.

7 Central nave. The vaults reach forty-five metres high.

8 Transept of the Passion side

Apse cupola

The Glory façade
Gaudí plans a platform that crosses over Mallorca Street.

Light diffusers
They cover the hollows in the vault, filtering zenithal light that streams through into the temple.

The temple's symbolic dimension

The interior of the Basilica of the Sagrada Familia is devoted to the exaltation of the universal Church and describes two paths that are crossed: the Path of Humanity – symbolised by the line that goes from the door of the Glory façade to the apse– and the Path of Jesus Christ, which represents the life of Jesus from his incarnation to his resurrection and goes from the Nativity façade to the Passion.

The five naves

Gaudí decided to increase the width of the temple to five naves in his first project and with the passing of the years he perfected on his structural proposal until devising, just before his death, the definitive layout.

Saint George
Patron Saint of Catalonia, the sculpture is work of Josep Maria Subirachs and is put on the inner face of the Glory façade, overlooking the interior of the basilica.

The central nave

With the aim to facilitate total vision of the temple's interior space, Gaudí decides to broaden the dimensions of the main nave –initially devised by architect Del Villar– and initially delimits them with two rows of six columns with the purpose of providing a bird's eye view and to focus the worshippers' attention on the high altar. He therefore designs the central nave to be 15 metres wide –double that of the lateral naves– and puts the vault over it at a height of 45 metres, equivalent to the total width of the temple. This way he manages a uniform and open space achieving the spacial integration he sought for the basilica's interior.

Columns and vaults
The architect devised the naves as a spiritual forest.

Saints
Each one of the columns is dedicated to a saint from the Catholic Church.

1

Gaudí's original model with the five naves

SANTA MARÍA DEL MAR
Gaudí was inspired by this Gothic basilica in Born, a Barcelona district, when planning Sagrada Familia's interior.

Arborescent columns

Hyperbolic vaults

1

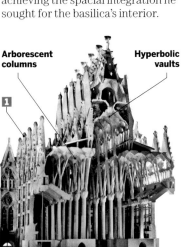

1987

Foundation work on the naves commences

1989

The columns and lateral walls of the temple are raised

1997

The lateral vaults are finished and the central ones are begun

1999

The central vaults are complete and the crossing is tackled

Stained glass
Work of Joan Vila-Grau, they provide colour and natural light to the naves.

2
Custodia over the choirstands

3
Lower stained glass windows of naves

Holy water font
It is a giant shell donated by the Philippine Republic.

1.200
PEOPLE
can gather in the adult choirstands that are located on the lateral naves.

The lateral naves

Gaudí devised the basilica's four lateral naves with the same harmonious proportions as the rest of the temple. With the intention of continuing with the general module concept, he designs each one of the secondary naves to be 7.5 metres wide –half that of the central nave– and 30 metres wide, equivalent to two-thirds of the main nave. However, the architect's greatest achievement in this section of the temple was to connect the structural and functional aspects. This way he positions the choirstands over two of the four lateral naves, making them rest on the shafts of the arborescent columns and the walls.

The choirstands. Gaudí puts the choirs in this section for two reasons: to make the most of the space and so the choir is near to worshippers.

Circulation around the basilica. In order to be able to guarantee correct, free and natural movement, whether for worshippers or clergy, throughout the different parts of the temple, Gaudí plans a system of winding staircases –two alongside the apse and the transept and two over the Glory's interior façade– and several corridors with the purpose of connecting the different areas of the basilica. To carry out this idea, the architect follows the classical guidelines of medieval cathedrals and creates a series of triforiums of differing height that go around most of the temple's perimeter.

The high altar and the baldachin

With the contributions that Gaudí makes to the crypt project, he manages to raise the height of the altar two metres above the level of the naves, this way achieving stronger presence and visibility from any point in the interior.

⬅ **Easter candelabra**
Designed by Gaudí himself in order to support the altar candle that is lit during the Christian Easter period, the wrought iron candelabra's shapes are taken from nature.

The central nucleus

As the main nucleus of the basilica, the altar is situated at the point where two of the temple's most important axis converge: on one side, the *via humanitatis*, which runs from the centre of the Glory façade until midway through the apse's central chapel, and, on the other, the line that goes through the crypt, the altar and Mary's cimborio –the tower that culminates the presbytery and tops the apse–, an axis that perpendicularly crosses the other path. Precisely in conjunction with this last imaginary line, the baldachin that covers the high altar, a structure inspired by the same element planned by Antoni Gaudí for Mallorca Cathedral in 1912. From the baldachin's framework hang Jesus' cross, the vine and wheat –symbol of the Eucharist– and fifty lights, in reference to Saint John Lateran's Basilica, which is Rome's cathedral.

1.90
METRES
is the image of the crucified Christ that hangs from the baldachin of the Sagrada Familia.

The baldachin from Mallorca
Gaudí did a similar work during the cathedral's refurbishment.

➡ **The presbytery**
The semicircle of columns mark the limits of the presbytery, in whose centre is the high altar.

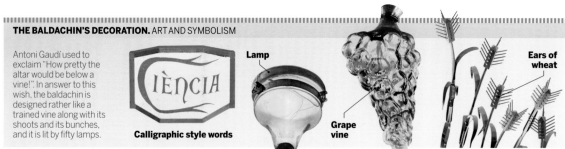

THE BALDACHIN'S DECORATION. ART AND SYMBOLISM

Antoni Gaudí used to exclaim "How pretty the altar would be below a vine!". In answer to this wish, the baldachin is designed rather like a trained vine along with its shoots and its bunches, and it is lit by fifty lamps.

Calligraphic style words

Lamp

Grape vine

Ears of wheat

The transept

The transverse nave, which with the longitudinal naves forms the Latin cross floor, links the Nativity with the Passion façade and represents the path taken by Jesus from Bethlehem up to his death and resurrection.

1
Saint Joseph
Situated on the Nativity side of the transept, the sculpture of the patron saint of the constructor association of the basilica was carried out by Catalan artist Ramon Cuello.

Colossal proportions

Antoni Gaudí remained faithful to his convictions and the evocation of medieval architectonic shapes that abounded in the latter half of the nineteenth century. This therefore led to his incorporation of a spacious transept with three naves, whose most important characteristic is its sixty metre height, where the vaults are located that cover the mentioned area and where the basilica's highest tower commences, the cimborio dedicated to Jesus Christ. Supported by twelve columns –four of which are the central pillars dedicated to the Evangelists that support the crossing's vault–, the transept designed by Antoni Gaudí is one of the largest transepts planned in the history of universal ecclesiastical architecture.

⊙
The transept's two wings
The Nativity's neo-Gothic interior contrasts with the angled lines of the Passion façade.

The tears
Gaudí situated them on the interior of the Nativity façade as a symbol of pain.

60
METRES
is the length of the transept from the Nativity façade to the Passion.

Walkway or triforium around the transept

Column
Gaudí left examples of how some structural elements should be sculpted.

Symbols of the Evangelists
The four columns on the crossing are adorned with some lights decorated with tetramorphs, the symbology of the four Evangelists, Matthew, Mark, Luke and John.

2 Virgin Mary
In travertine stone by sculptor Ramon Cuello, it presides over the Passion side.

Holy Family symbol
In *trencadís*, the initials of Jesus, Mary and Joseph make up the symbol.

Interior wall of the Passion façade

The two interior façades

The north-east south-west orientation of the transept –facing dawn and dusk– is essential in order to illuminate the basilica. Thanks to this layout, as much the openings made in the mentioned walls as the stained glass that covers them carry out a triple function: to light up the temple during the early and late hours of the day, to propose a different and alternative aesthetic solution for each one of the two interior walls with a circular rose window on the east façade and oval one on the west– and to function as a base for a specific symbolic program: the eastern wing is dedicated to Saint Joseph and the western wing, to Mary.

CHRIST'S PATHWAY. THE TRANSEPT

The transept symbolises the Stations of the Cross, the path of the Messiah from his birth (east wing) up to his Passion, death and resurrection (west wing).

Nativity arrangement

Crucifixion sculpture

The arborescent columns

The spiritual forest that Gaudí wanted to build inside the Sagrada Familia became reality thanks to the arborescent columns, a revolutionary structure in the history of architecture.

Nature as a model

Gaudí investigated for years until he managed to come up with a column that avoided the use of buttresses on walls. Loyal to the teachings of nature, two years before his death, in the year 1924, he was sufficiently inspired to find a definitive solution: the arborescent column. The architect wanted the pillars supporting the temple to combine the strength and beauty of the largest trees. For this reason he fled from the rigid verticality of classical architectonic references and designed columns that tilted in relation to the height they reached in order that they could withstand the loads originating from the roof. The secret lay in turning the column's shaft in two directions – as happens with trees– in order to achieve a better resistance and by branching out the upper section into small columns in order that the nave vaults are adequately supported.

36
COLUMNS
of diverse heights and thickness are those that support the interior structure of the Sagrada Familia.

The capitals
Gaudí stylized to the maximum the union between columns and vaults with his idea of emulating a forest.

 Preliminary studies
Gaudí carried out some experiments with tilted and helicoidal columns in Park Güell.

Node and light

Concave grooves

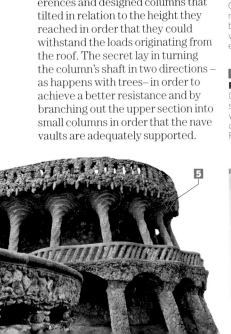

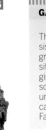

GAUDÍ. STUDIES

The model of analysis of the organic growth of plants is situated in the origin of the definitive solution for the columns of the Basilica of the Sagrada Familia.

Mateu

1

Thickness and material

Gaudí planned columns of various material according to the weight supported. On the crossing he had thicker ones made, of porphyry, and on the lateral naves, the lighter ones, with stone from Montjuïc.

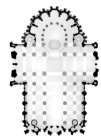

1

Porphyry columns

They support the vault over the crossing and are twelve-sided with a 2.10 metre diameter.

2

Basalt columns

Very resistant ,they have a 1.75 metre diameter and a section comprising of 10 sides.

3

Granite columns

Of a blueish grey colour, they boast a 1.40 metre diameter and a section comprising of eight sides.

4

Columns of Montjuïc stone

They are the lightest and have a diameter of 1.05 metres and six sides.

The columns of the neo-Gothic project
Gaudí devised Gothic columns for the first project of the basilica.

THE STRUCTURE

A revolutionary solution

The tree-shape pillars were the solution that Gaudí planned for the structure of the temple.

Branches

Nature as master
The architect was greatly inspired by the shape of tree trunks when planning the design of the columns.

Columns

15 metres

Relieving the load
The series of lines of varying inclination help absorb the weight of the vaults on one point.

The vaults

Gaudí takes elements from Gothic art and from traditional Catalan architecture and applies to them what he has learnt from his patient observation of nature, devising new, never seen before structures.

Roof

Central vault
It rises 45 metres above the nave floor.

Lateral vaults
Made from concrete, they rise thirty metres above the paving of the lateral naves.

The end of Gaudí's path

Supported by arborescent columns that branch out high up in the basilica, the vaults that cover the naves and the transept represent the culmination of Gaudí's artistic evolution from the modernized neo-Gothic forms of his first project up to the application of the so-called double-ruled surfaces, in this case hyperboloid ones. Light and very easy for light to penetrate through, the interior roof is a sumptuous version of the Catalan bricked vault technique. Widely used in the territory, this highly valued, traditional construction technique is normally devised using solid brickwork, but for the building work on the basilica, it was designed with reinforced concrete on the lateral naves – forming a star-like design– and with ceramic tiles on the central nave, creating a helicoidal layout similar to palm leaves.

1924
IS THE YEAR
Antoni Gaudí conceives using hyperbolic vaults instead of ribbed ones.

Catalan vault
Antoni Gaudí reinterpreted the traditional system of the brick vault for the roof of the central nave.

The vaults of the lateral naves
The branching out of the columns support the original, star-shaped vaults.

VAULT MODULATION. PREFABRICATED WITH REINFORCED CONCRETE

The interior roof of the lateral naves of the basilica is carried out in reinforced concrete in accordance with Gaudí's original plans. The architect foresaw a system of prefabricated modules that, joined together, make up the starred shapes of the vaults of this sector.

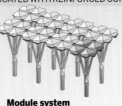
Module system

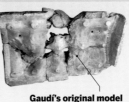
Gaudí's original model

Gaudí's model

Natural light

One of Gaudí's main concerns at the moment of lightening the walls and the vaults of the temple was to facilitate the entrance of light –the main symbol of Jesus Christ– into the basilica by means of numerous openings.

Precursors of the stained glass
With Sagrada Familia in mind, Gaudí implemented his new ideas in other works, such is the case of the Cathedral of Palma de Mallorca.

A temple invaded by light

The sturdiness of the load-bearing structure devised by Gaudí after decades of study meant that large zenithal claraboyas of hyperboloid form could be included in the vaults that, along with the enormous hollows made in the walls, illuminate the interior in a harmonious and uniform manner. The diffusers that the architect planned to cover these large openings in the temple's roof allow natural light to filter through which achieves an atmosphere ideal for retreat and prayer in the enormous space occupied by the naves. In the same way, the ogival windows and rose windows of neo-Gothic genre that go round the temple were planned by Gaudí in order to hold a new type of stained glass, with a system created by the architect that consists of superimposing three panes of primary colours, resulting in a combination of new tones.

Stained glass variegates natural light

1999

IS THE YEAR
artist Joan Vila-Grau takes on the design of the temple's stained glass windows.

JOAN VILA-GRAU

Expert in liturgical art, this Barcelonan painter and glazier collaborated with artist Joan Miró.

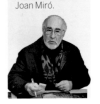

Rose window

A claraboya in a vault

Upper windows

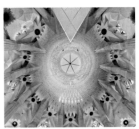
Altar vault

Stained glass work. Abstract forms abound in Joan Vila-Grau's work for the Sagrada Familia, an artist that combines a reticle of lead based on straight lines with curved shapes that mark the composition and lend it dynamism. In front of this abstraction, Vila-Grau skilfully selects a wide range of colours and tones for each window, avoiding the mix of cold and warm tones that characterize medieval stained glass windows and helping to create an almost supernatural atmosphere thanks to the warmth of the light and the reflection of the drawings on the temple's walls.

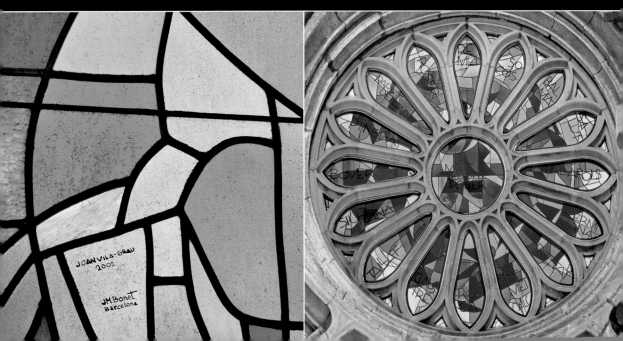

Artificial light

Gaudí was concerned that dusk and night time celebrations be provided with a light that would come as close as possible in quantity, quality and tones to the natural light that entered the temple during the day.

Study of illumination
Lights of hyperboloid profile illuminate the basilica from the height of the nodes on the columns, creating an atmosphere for meditation.

Warm and subdued lighting

Despite the technical limitations of the early 20th century, Gaudí envisaged light sources that were able to maintain the same harmony obtained during the day with windows and claraboyas. To do so, he wanted the light given off to be filtered by diffusers to provide warmth and subtlety to the illumination.

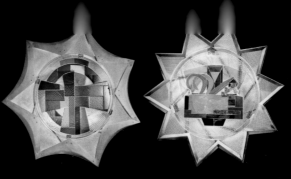

The vault's light diffusers

Decorated with Christian symbols, the diffusers positioned in the openings of the vaults of the naves have the double function of filtering light from the exterior and projecting artificial light.

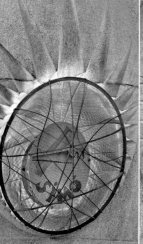

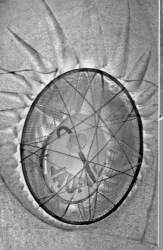

The exterior walls

Unburdened by the buttresses that reinforced the structure of medieval cathedrals, the walls of the Sagrada Familia offer a good part of their surface area to the light that comes through the large windows.

Six stretches either side

Each one of the two walls that laterally close the temple is formed by the repetition of a stretch composed of two superimposed ogival windows and a triangular pediment that tops it. This module is repeated six times on each side, five along the lateral naves and one more on a right angle, following the profile of the transept. Antoni Gaudí's designs for this sector of the temple show the evolution of the architect from the purely neo-Gothic forms of the late nineteenth century, evident on the windows of the lower section, to the personal style that can be observed on the upper pediments, marked by the elliptically-shaped central opening, designs devised by Gaudí during the last years of his life. This last solution is also employed on the central nave's walls, situated in the background, reaching a height of around seventy metres.

The central and lateral nave walls

1
Alpha and omega
The Greek alphabet's first and last letter symbolise Jesus as Beginning and End.

2
The walls' first stretch
On the lower windows, Gaudí used the neo-Gothic style that was popular in the early 20th century.

3
Second solution for the walls
Over time, the architect evolves to a style of clearly geometric shapes.

4
Christian allegory
A censer accompanies the Latin word *thur* –incense– on the drains of the walls.

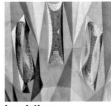

Work symbols
In the image and likeness of medieval cathedrals.

Allegories
Legends decorate the union of the drains and walls.

Water drains
Pyramidal shapes combine aesthetics and function.

Inscriptions
Carried out based on *trencadís* Venetian glass work.

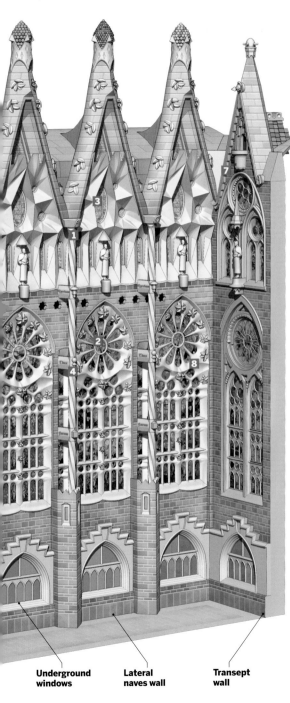

Third solution for the walls
More simplified they have a clearly geometric style.

Symbol of Jesus
The initial *J* that identifies the Son of God is shown sculpted in relief.

34
METRES
is the height that the Sagrada Familia's lateral naves' walls arrive at.

Fruit trees
The naves' walls have decorative carvings with their inspiration taken from nature.

Christian symbology
The naves' exterior walls, for not having buttresses to support them, have a diaphanous surface area only reserved for large windows and the decorative program conceived by Gaudí, packed with Christian symbology, such as the images of founding saints, inscriptions and allegorical words from liturgy, and the fruit baskets that top the windows and which symbolise the goods of the Holy Spirit.

Underground windows **Lateral naves wall** **Transept wall**

SCULPTURE. THE FOUNDING SAINTS

Gaudí suggested putting sculptures of the founding saints of the main religious orders on each stretch of wall, between the ogival windows and the pediments.

Saint John Bosco

Joaquina de Vedruna

Saint José Oriol

The Holy Spirit and the Eucharist. As decorative ending of the windows of the central and lateral nave of the basilica, Gaudí placed two groups of symbolic elements. In the first group, located on the pinnacles of the windows of the lateral nave, he included the symbology of the Holy Spirit, represented by spring, summer, autumn and winter fruits. The second group, located on the pinnacles of the windows of the central nave, he used it to symbolise the Eucharist, represented by ears of wheat and the sacred shape, and the bunches of grapes and the chalice or pyx.

07 | ANTONI GAUDÍ'S FINAL WORK
The Nativity façade

The eastern side of the basilica is the model left by the architect to the constructors that carry on with his work.

"It just isn't possible for one sole generation to erect the entire temple. Let's therefore leave behind a vigorous display of our passage, in order that future generations are encouraged to do the same". With these words Gaudí conveyed a combination of modesty, pragmatism and a command of the history of art, by foreseeing that the construction of the Sagrada Familia would follow the same pace as the great medieval cathedrals and which he would only get to see just started. This vigorous display that the architect referred to was the Nativity façade, whose construction work lasted 41 years and was completed in 1936 –ten years after the accidental death of the artist– with the culmination of the pinnacles of the three portals that make it up. This façade is the only part of the basilica that Gaudí totally designed and which he got to see almost finished, with the re-sult that it has converted into the most Gaudían universal paradigm of the Sagrada Familia, achieving the goal set by the architect when planning it: to serve as an example in order that those who continue on with his work may observe the sculptural and decorative terminations that he envisaged for the totality of the work. If this has been made possible, it is largely thanks to the donations of well-to-do Barcelonan families which allowed Gaudí to realize the complex decorative program that he had devised for the façade. Another influencing factor was the determination of the work's administrator, who pressured the architect to rapidly invest the money in models and material, artists and the workmen necessary to raise the façade, before the bishop and the Barcelonan diocese could spread donations out amongst other projects, common practice at the time.

 The Hope portico
The doorway on the left sector of the Nativity façade is dedicated to Saint Joseph as Patron Saint of the Catholic Church.

Wrought iron
The façade's decorative program is completed with the ornamentation of the gate separating the street and entrance steps.

Iron sheeting

The triumph of life

Facing the East and divided into three porticos, the Nativity façade explains the main facts about the early years of Jesus Christ's life in a sculptural and ornamental context packed with optimism and vitality.

Three porticos below four towers

Although Gaudí considered the Gothic as an "imperfect" genre, with the Nativity façade he followed a scheme typical of this style and structured it around three porticos -a central one and two lateral ones- accompanied by four bell towers on the eastern side and lodged in the hollows of these towers' bases. The architect dedicated them to the three members of the Holy Family, each linked to a theological virtue: the portico on the left represents Hope, a virtue associated to Saint Joseph; the central one, dedicated to Jesus, represents Charity, which is topped by a naturalist pinnacle –The Tree of Life– which competes in height with the towers: and the portico on the right represents Faith, personified by the Virgin Mary.

Josep Maria Jujol's model. The architect, Gaudí's apprentice carried out paint samples with the intention of polychroming the façade.

🔄 **Snow on stone**
Some decorative elements on the façade were covered by snow, an element that reminds of the festive season.

1 THE HOPE PORTICO

2 THE CHARITY PORTICO

3 THE FAITH PORTICO

✳ **The façade**
The porticos are lodged in the more concave shapes of the base of the towers.

The Faith pinnacle

Lateral balconies

CHRONOLOGY. THE EVOLUTION OF THE FAÇADE

1896
Building work advances
Two years after the foundations are laid, the pillars start to take shape.

1899
The porticos' structure
In this year the base of the façade can be seen, with the porticos practically finished.

1920
The bell towers' base
Six years before Gaudí's death, only the façade towers had to be finished off.

The towers' spires

Bell towers

4
The Tree of Life
It culminates the Charity portico at a great height and symbolises eternal life.

1936
IS THE YEAR
in which the structure of the façade is concluded with the inclusion of the Tree of Life.

Living beings
A large quantity of animals and plants are carved in stone on the façade.

2005
IS THE YEAR
in which UNESCO declares the Nativity façade a World Heritage Site.

5
Mary's pinnacle
It is the culminating point of the Faith portico and holds an image of the Virgin Mary.

The Charity portico

The Hope portico

The Faith portico

Jesus' early years
The façade explains the episodes related to the conception, birth, childhood and adolescence of Jesus, from the Annunciation up to his meeting with the scholars in the temple. The sculptors commissioned to bring Gaudí's ideas to life depict the more human side to the Son of God with scenes of joy, tenderness and dynamism, with the aim to exalt Creation: Nature in all its splendour seems to celebrate the arrival of the Messiah. In order to bring the sculptural groups nearer to worshippers, the architect incorporated popular resources –tools from trades and domestic animals– which any citizen of the time would have been able to identify with.

The Virgin Mary's sign

Jesus' sign

Joseph's sign

The monumental columns

The three porticos on the temple's east façade are separated by two attached columns of palm tree shape and culminated by pairs of trumpeteering angels that announce the birth of Jesus.

Bronze trumpet

Angel of the Saint Joseph column

Carved stone

Between heaven and earth

Despite being just a side entrance to the basilica, Antoni Gaudí positioned two monumental columns on the Nativity façade –in the style of the main entrances of great temples– and arranged them separating the three porticos that make it up. Attached to the wall the columns possess a very tall trunk with spiralling indents and in the centre have much wider carved stone decorated with plant motifs that incorporate the names of the figures to whom they are dedicated: Saint Joseph is on the left and the Virgin Mary is on the right. Both columns represent the connection between the secular world and the heavenly world and are finished off by naturalist capitals that emulate palm leaves from which grow numerous bunches of dates and which provide support for the trumpeting angels that culminate the arrangement.

The angels of the Nativity
The angels blow their bronze trumpets announcing the coming of the Son of God to Earth.

1
The spheres
The herald angels stand on spheres that symbolise the light of the sun.

1899

IS THE YEAR
the sculptures of the trumpeteering angels are put into place on the Nativity façade of the basilica.

THE SCULPTOR. LLORENÇ MATAMALA

Gaudí's close friend, Llorenç Matamala (1856-1925) was in charge of the temple's sculptors and creator of many of the façade's sculptural groups, such as the Trumpeteering Angels, the Death of the Innocents, the Flight to Egypt, Saint Joseph's boat, Jesus the Carpenter or the Immaculate Conception.

Instrument symbol of the Word of God

➔ **The Nativity façade in 1897**
The carving of sculptures was carried out at the same time as the architectonic construction work on the façade.

Bunches of dates with snow

Capital
At the feet of the angels, the snow that overflows from high mixes with a typically tropical element, such as palm leaves.

➔ **Joseph's column**
It is situated between the Hope and the Charity porticos.

13.5
METRES
is the total height reached by the attached columns of the Nativity façade.

Saint Joseph's inscription
The central cylinder shows whom the column is dedicated to.

The shaft
The spiral fluting reminds of the solomonic columns found in the Temple of Jerusalem.

The Angels of the Nativity
Each column supports two angels, simply dressed and –as all angels on the façade– wingless, who announce the birth of Jesus with their bronze trumpets. The models for the carvings, work of sculptor Llorenç Matamala, were three military musicians and Ricard Opisso, Gaudí's collaborator and well-known illustrator.

Capital with palm leaves

The inscription of the Virgin
Mary's column separates the Charity and the Faith porticos.

The tortoises
The column which is nearest to the mountain rests on the top of a tortoise.

Sea turtle

Column base

The Hope portico

Dedicated to Saint Joseph and located in the left-hand sector of the façade, the Hope portico shows several scenes from the life of the Holy Family that convey the value of this virtue in times of adversity.

Mountainous and fluvial

Although it does not reach the height of the central portal, the Hope portico combines some marked vertical proportions, which are exemplary for displaying the mountainous surroundings that are inspired by the massif of Montserrat, and a context of flora and aquatic fauna that reminds of the banks of the River Nile, in consonance with one of the main scenes represented: the Holy Family fleeing from Egypt after an angel appears in Joseph's dreams, warning him of the Slaughter of the Innocents. This last biblical fact, also shown on the portico, makes up the goriest sculptural group on the whole façade.

1
Betrothal of the Virgin Mary and Saint Joseph

High priest

5
SCULPTURAL GROUPS
decorate the portico, as well as other works in stone.

1935
IS THE YEAR
in which the last sculptures on the Hope portico were finally completed.

✱
The holy mountain
Gaudí refers to the Mountain of Montserrat, where the image of the Patron Saint of Catalonia is found.

Blocks of stone

The prayer
On the pinnacle of the portico Gaudí put the prayer 'Sálvanos'.

Refuge of the Holy Family

PINNACLE

PORTAL

➲
Flight to Egypt
An angel guides the Holy Family whilst Mary looks after Jesus.

6
Chameleons
They symbolise constant change, in contrast to the turtles.

5
The rosary
Fifty-nine beads go around the windows of the portico.

3 Tools

4 Fauna on the Nile

5 Rosary beads

6 Chameleon

7
The Slaughter of the Innocents
Llorenç Matamala depicted the scene of a Roman soldier murdering a child.

3
METRES
is the height of the dramatic sculpture of the Slaughter of the Innocents.

Six toes
One of the soldier's feet have six toes in reference to monstrosity.

Mother defending her offspring

Roman soldier

Cloak or paenula

Two newly bornes lay dead at the feet of a soldier

Family scenes
In the context of sculptural groups related to Jesus' childhood, the tympanum of the Hope portico represents a very tender scene: Jesus shows his father Saint Joseph a wounded dove, which symbolises the Holy Spirit, while Saint Joachim and Saint Anne, his grandparents, emotionally look on.

8 **9** **10**

Jesus' family. Work of Llorenç Matamala following Gaudí's composition, the sculptural group is framed by a rosary.

DESTRUCTION. THE CIVIL WAR

The Nativity façade underwent serious damage during the anti-clerical riots which took place at the very start of the Spanish Civil War, in July 1936.

Saint Joseph's pinnacle

The crags inspired by Montserrat, Catalonia's sacred mountain, are the setting for the boat of Saint Joseph, who is Patron Saint of the Church and of the promoting institution of the expiatory temple.

'Save us'
The rocky crags that cover the sculptural group of the boat of Saint Joseph are engraved with the motto 'Save us' with stone relief letters, in a message of hope.

The helm of the Catholic Church

To go under the crags that culminate the Hope portico, Gaudí had Llorenç Matamala's studio create the figure of Saint Joseph navigating a boat, a vessel that symbolises the passage of the Catholic Church, whose helmsman is the patriarch of the Holy Family and father of the Church. The cave the boat crosses and the darkness surrounding it represents the difficulties that Saint Joseph will face on his way, while the underground waters that the boat sails through stand for spiritual purity and regeneration. The fact that this imaginary river flows below a sculptural piece inspired by the rounded shapes of the Massif of Montserrat is interpreted as a homage to the Patron Saint of Catalonia, whose Romanesque carving was found by some young shepherds inside a cave in the above mentioned mountainous zone, near Barcelona.

38 METRES
is the total height of the Hope portico, from ground level to the pinnacle.

Montserrat
Gaudí was inspired by this Barcelonan rocky massif for the top of the portico.

Saint Joseph
The likeness to Gaudí is an apparent homage by the workers of the temple following his death.

SYMBOLOGY. THE ELEMENTS OF SAINT JOSEPH'S BOAT

Four symbolic objects decorate Saint Joseph's boat: the helm to navigate the vessel successfully; the dove –the Holy Spirit– on the canopy, symbolic of Noah's Ark; the anchor of the solidness of the Church; and the lantern, symbol of the Word of Jesus Christ.

Boat helm

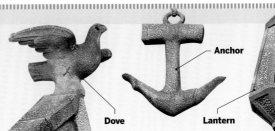

Dove

Anchor

Lantern

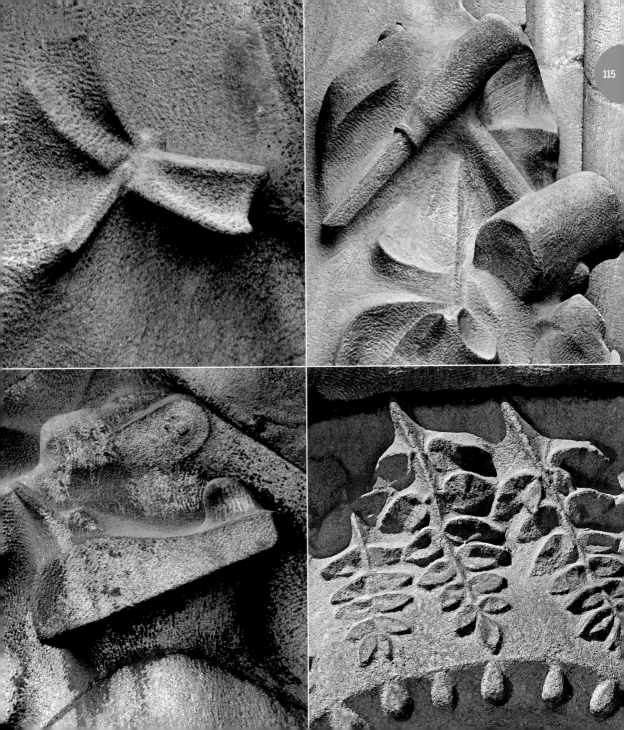

The Charity portico

With the sculptural group of the Nativity in the centre of the composition, the Charity portico is a tribute to joy, generosity and altruism, palpable virtues in all the carvings of the arrangement.

Joy in a Bethlehem stable

Dedicated to Jesus and to the third theological virtue –the other two are Faith and Hope, the Charity portico takes up the central and largest space of the Nativity façade. Practically indiscernible due to the sculptural and ornamental detail that Gaudí devised for the main entrance to the temple from the eastern side, the walls of this portico create a concave space that generates a large scale cave that depicts the stable scene where the Messiah was born. Moreover, the sculptural groups on this portico display the different protagonists that are associated with the birth of Jesus with up to thirty-three human figures depicted in stone, as well as a large number of plants and domestic animals –particularly birds– which contribute with their aura of innocence to the celebration of the arrival of the Messiah.

1
Chorus of young angels. Sculptural group by Etsuro Sotoo.

2
Musicians. Sotoo represented the angels playing instruments from popular and religious music.

THE RESTORATION. SCULPTOR ETSURO SOTOO

Since 1978 Japanese sculptor Etsuro Sotoo has collaborated on the restoration of the sculptural groups on the façade, many of which were destroyed during the Civil War, in the year 1936.

Restoration process

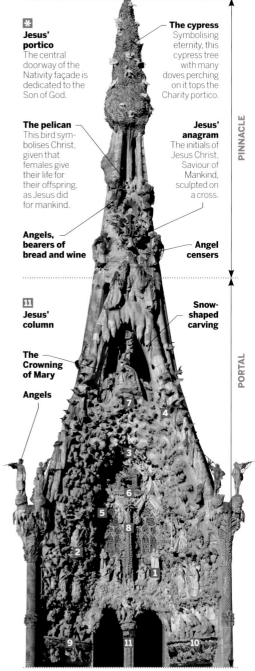

✳ Jesus' portico
The central doorway of the Nativity façade is dedicated to the Son of God.

The pelican
This bird symbolises Christ, given that females give their life for their offspring, as Jesus did for mankind.

Angels, bearers of bread and wine

The cypress
Symbolising eternity, this cypress tree with many doves perching on it tops the Charity portico.

Jesus' anagram
The initials of Jesus Christ, Saviour of Mankind, sculpted on a cross.

Angel censers

PINNACLE

11 Jesus' column

The Crowning of Mary

Angels

Snow-shaped carving

PORTAL

3
Signs of the zodiac

4
Nature

5
The rosary

The Annunciation
This work by sculptor Jaume Busquets shows the moment that the archangel Gabriel tells Mary that she has been chosen to bring the Son of God into the world.

6

7

The Crowning of the Virgin Mary
Work of Joan Matamala, Llorenç Matamala's son, it depicts the moment that the Virgin is crowned as recompense for her selfless love of God.

Mary
She bows to Jesus when crowned Queen of Heaven and Earth.

The crown
Its metal sheen contrasts with the matt and ochre tones of the façade stone.

Saint Joseph

The Holy Spirit

Scenes from the Virgin's life

Although the portico arrangement is dedicated to Jesus, Mary is the protagonist of diverse sculptural groups on the portal, such as the Annunciation, situated above the ogival windows that provide the transept with light, and the Coronation, high up in the portico and protected by a large, catenary shaped niche of Gaudían style, which frames and highlights the scene before the absence of other sculptures surrounding it.

The Star of Bethlehem
The sign from the sky that announces the arrival of the Messiah projects upwards and its tail points to the Holy Family.

2000
IS THE YEAR
the reconstruction of the singing angels on the Charity portico was finalized, carried out by Japanese sculptor Etsuro Sotoo.

8

9
The Adoration of the Magi

10
The Adoration of the Shepherds

Jesus' column

The main entrance to inside the temple via the Nativity façade is by means of a portal divided into two arches by a mullion that supports the Holy Family group.

Wingless angels
None of the many angels that are represented on the Nativity façade were sculpted with wings, as Antoni Gaudí argued that angels were unable to fly.

Around the Nativity

Gaudí had the sculptural arrangement of the Nativity put into place – symbolic centre of the façade of the same name– over the column of the mullion of the Charity portico that precedes the entrance to the basilica interior. However, it wasn't until the 19th of March 1958 –Saint Joseph's Day– when the definitive arrangement was installed, work of sculptor Jaume Busquets, modernist artist Joan Llimona's apprentice and, from an early age, Gaudí's too. The composition created by Busquets, with the ox and mule surrounding the Nativity scene, focuses the spectator's attention on the figure of the Child – at the same time protected and exhibited by the Virgin– and carries out the function of focal point amongst surrounding sculptures.

3 The Nativity
Over the capital of the column is Jesus accompanied by Joseph and Mary surrounded by the ox and the mule.

Joseph standing

1958
IS THE YEAR in which the Nativity group was put into place, work of Catalan sculptor named Jaume Busquets.

SCULPTURE STUDY
Jaume Busquets carried out the model of the Nativity sculpture in terracotta.

Mary with Jesus

The ox

4 "Gloria in excelsis Deo". On the upper part of the doors is the phrase spoken by the angel to the shepherds in order to announce the Birth.

Pedestal of support

Nativity animals
The ox and mule surround the Holy Family in the arrangement of the Birth of Christ.

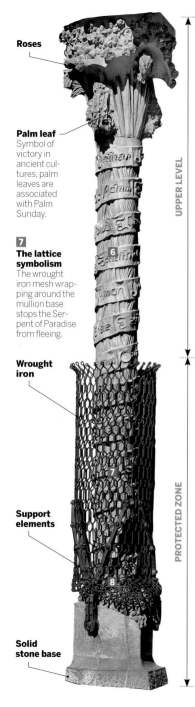

Roses

Palm leaf
Symbol of victory in ancient cultures, palm leaves are associated with Palm Sunday.

7
The lattice symbolism
The wrought iron mesh wrapping around the mullion base stops the Serpent of Paradise from fleeing.

Wrought iron

Support elements

Solid stone base

UPPER LEVEL

PROTECTED ZONE

5
METRES
is how high Jesus' column reaches, the mullion of the façade's main entrance.

The name of Jesus
The inscription can be seen high up on the capital at the foot of the Nativity group.

Dates
Fruits from the palm tree hang from the capital of the column dedicated to Jesus.

40
NAMES
from Jesus' genealogy decorate the shaft of the mullion of the Charity portico.

8
The serpent
The reptile with the apple in the base of the column symbolises original sin.

The mullion divides the Charity's portal into two archways.

Jesus' column
Finished off by a capital with intricate floral decoration that supports the depiction of the Nativity, the mullion or column that divides the main entrance has a ribbon twisting around it in which Jesus' genealogy is detailed, while on the base a serpent that can be seen biting an apple symbolises the original sin.

Jesus' genealogy
The ribbon around the column names Jesus' predecessors dating from Abraham.

SYMBOLISM. THE SERPENT AND THE ORIGINAL SIN

Gaudí represented the symbolism of the serpent and the apple via the mullion as he wanted to situate the original sin in the origin of the Birth of Jesus; precisely the existence of the sin was the cause for God to become Man.

'The Original Sin', by Michelangelo

The signs of the zodiac
The vault over the Annunciation depicts the
constellations just as they were the night that
Jesus was born.

Nature on the portico

Receiving the morning sun that lends it symbolic vitality, the Nativity façade, and the Charity portico in particular, display a blossoming of life that accompanies the celebration of the Coming of the Messiah.

⊖
Plant shapes
The depiction of fauna on the Nativity façade enables the creation of a plastic setting that serves as a nexus between the different sculptural groups.

Warmth and symbolism

For the decoration of the Charity portico Antoni Gaudí devised a clearly defined program that was based on impact and symbolism. In order to carry off his scheme he decides to smother the walls with biblical representations associated with Jesus' life and above all Christmas traditions, a setting that provides warmth and popularity to the decorative program. In this sense, each representation responds to a defined symbolism: the birds, due to their ability to fly, are messengers between Heaven and Earth, in contrast to the serpent, who embodies all that is terrestrial. The abundance of flowers, in contrast, represents the blossoming of springtime, associated with the birth of a new cycle, while the cypress tree that dominates the portico symbolises the passing of time and the doves allude to the presence of the Holy Spirit.

18
SPECIES
of different types of plants and flowers can be located on the Charity portico.

Squirrel
Apart from domestic animals, the façade includes species of wild fauna.

⊖
Close up of flora
Flowers surge in relief form from the stone, creating delicate chiaroscuros on the façade walls.

TRADITION. DOMESTIC AND FARM ANIMALS

In his wish to connect the iconography of the façade to Christmas celebrations, Gaudí had various examples of farm and domestic animals sculpted, many of which are related to the traditional Nativity scenes that are recreated throughout Catalonia.

Turkey

Duck

Dog

Lamb

Birds
Birds emerge from the Charity portico from all directions, representing the message that is sent down from Heaven to terrestrial Earth.

The angel musicians

Surrounding the Nativity's central scene, slightly higher up, a chorus of young angels celebrate the good news accompanied by six musicians that play instruments used in religious and popular music.

Popular instruments
Three of the angel musicians play instruments from popular music: the guitar, bagpipes and tambourine, chosen to bring the scene closer to the tastes of worshippers from humble backgrounds.

Music on stone

Apart from devising a celestial court around the recently born Jesus, Gaudí aspired, with a combination of classical and popular instruments, to represent all types of music –and from all social classes– and to add the auditary sensation to the celebration of the senses which the Nativity façade converted into.

The chorus of singing angels

The original sculptures were made from plaster and destroyed in 1936. Today's works are an interpretation by Japanese sculptor Etsuro Sotoo parting from the ideas that Gaudí left behind.

The Tree of Life

In contrast to the general simplicity of the biblical motifs chosen for the sculptural decoration of the façade, the towering pinnacle that finishes off the Charity portico is the symbolic synthesis created for the whole ensemble.

Symbol of eternity

Gaudí reserved the top part of the portico for the representation of the Tree of Life, symbolic compendium of the three porticos that make up the Nativity façade and allegory of the triumph of Jesus' legacy. The tree, a cypress, symbolises eternity due to the evergreen of its leaves and its hard-wearing wood. Its green shade stands out from the stone context of the façade, hinting at the effect that would have been created by the application of the idea Gaudí had deliberated over for many years: to polychrome all the sculptural elements of the basilica. The architect had the cypress crowned with the sign of the Holy Trinity and proposed a total of twenty-one white alabaster doves fluttering around the tree; at its base is a pelican, a Eucharist symbol that feeds its offspring and which is situated between two ladders of six rungs that represent the aspiration of reaching eternal life.

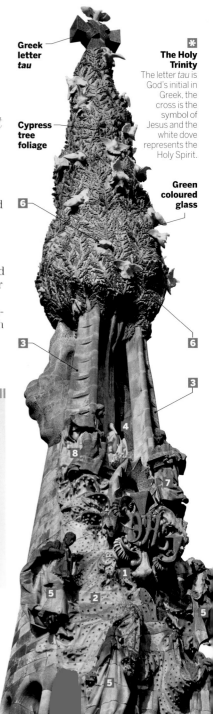

Greek letter *tau*

Cypress tree foliage

✳ **The Holy Trinity**
The letter *tau* is God's initial in Greek, the cross is the symbol of Jesus and the white dove represents the Holy Spirit.

Green coloured glass

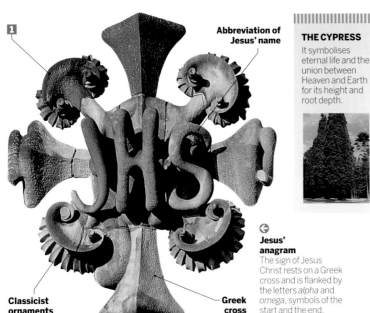

Abbreviation of Jesus' name

Classicist ornaments

Greek cross

‖‖‖‖‖‖‖‖‖‖‖‖‖‖‖‖‖‖‖‖

THE CYPRESS
It symbolises eternal life and the union between Heaven and Earth for its height and root depth.

↻ **Jesus' anagram**
The sign of Jesus Christ rests on a Greek cross and is flanked by the letters *alpha* and *omega*, symbols of the start and the end.

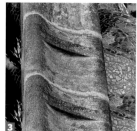

2
Incense
Small bubbles of incense go around Jesus' anagram.

3
The stairs
The two stairs resting on the cypress represent the aspiration to reach God.

4
Eucharist symbol
In ancient times it was believed that the pelican opened its chest to feed its young, for which it was associated with the Eucharist.

White marble
The pelican's original sculpture, of alabaster, was substituted by the present day one.

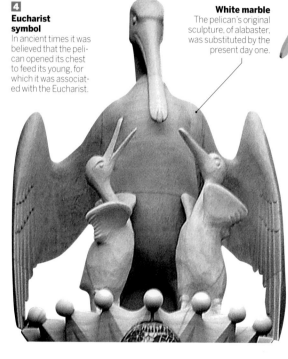

6
Doves
The original alabaster ones were substituted by marble ones.

21
DOVES
flutter around the Tree of Life that towers over the Nativity façade's Charity portico.

The egg
It symbolises the universe's origin and is engraved with Jesus Christ's anagram.

The angels with censers
Sign of purification, these angels that are situated below the cypress scatter holy smoke by swaying their censers.

THE EUCHARIST
Angels bearing bread and wine

These sculptures situated at the foot of the Tree of Life are one of the few sculptural arrangements shaped by Gaudí himself.

Angel bearer of bread

7

Sculpture work of Gaudí

8

1927
IS THE YEAR
Llorenç Matamala, chief sculptor, passes away, just one year after Antoni Gaudí.

Angel bearing wine
Carrying an amphora filled with Christ's blood converted into wine.

Study carried out by Gaudí

Colour scheme. Such as is demonstrated in many documents that are kept in the temple, left behind by Gaudí or by his collaborators, the architect intended to polychrome the entire Nativity façade. In this sense, the Tree of Life that tops the Charity portico is an example of how the vast surface area would have looked with colour: the green leaves of the cypress tree contrast with the red ceramic *trencadís* of the cross that finishes off the ensemble and with the white of the recently restored marble doves.

The Faith portico

Located on the far right hand side of the Nativity façade, it is dedicated to the Virgin Mary, but the protagonist of the majority of scenes is her son –infant and adolescent– Jesus.

1
The Visitation
This sculptural group situated to the left of the portal depicts the scene of Mary's visit, pregnant with Jesus, to her cousin Elizabeth, pregnant with Saint John the Baptist.

The Virgin and Jesus

In homage to the Virgin, Gaudí had sculptural groups of the Immaculate Conception and the Visitation to Saint Elizabeth sculpted, paradigms of the faith with which Mary assumed the divine plans, main symbolic motif on the portico. Other sculptural groups describe scenes related to the Son of God: the presentation of Jesus in the Temple of Jerusalem –a ritual of initiation that Hebrew parents used to carry out with their newly born children– and the preaching of Jesus in the same temple, provoking the admiration of his own parents, who observe him from lower down. However, the image that produces a closeness for its size, simplicity and naturalness is the daily representation of Jesus working as a carpenter.

2
Jesus the carpenter
Llorenç Matamala sculpted the scene of the Son of God helping his father in his workshop.

Work table

3

Joseph and Mary
Jesus' parents look on surprised at the prediction of the Messiah in the Temple of Jerusalem.

Jesus carrying out daily tasks

Posture
In this sculpture Jesus' humanity is paid more attention to than his divine status.

Support base

The chameleon. This reptile appears at the far ends of the façade and symbolises permanent change for it ability to change colour.

Sculpture study
A sample for the Jesus the Carpenter piece in the basilica's workshop.

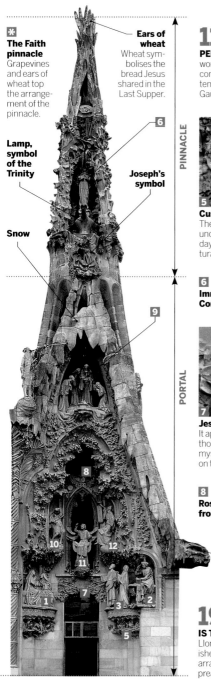

The Faith pinnacle
Grapevines and ears of wheat top the arrangement of the pinnacle.

Lamp, symbol of the Trinity

Snow

Ears of wheat
Wheat symbolises the bread Jesus shared in the Last Supper.

Joseph's symbol

PINNACLE

PORTAL

112
PEOPLE
worked in 1897 on the construction of the temple, under Antoni Gaudí's command.

5
Customs
The farm animals underline the everydayness of the sculptural scenes.

6
Immaculate Conception

7
Jesus' heart
It appears covered in thorns along with mystic bees that feast on the blood.

8
Rosaries hanging from the vault

1929
IS THE YEAR
Llorenç Matamala finishes the sculptural arrangement of Jesus preaching.

9 Jesus in Simeon's arms. The group of the Presentation of Jesus in the Temple depicts the Messiah in Priest Simeon's arms.

Saint John the Baptist   **Jesus**   **Saint Zachariah**

10   **11**   **12**

Jesus praying in the temple. Saint John, Jesus' cousin, and Saint Zachariah, father of the former, surround the Messiah in admiring attitude.

DOORS. WORKS BY ETSURO SOTOO

Designed by sculptor Etsuro Sotoo, the doors on the Nativity façade are polychrome bronze and reproduce plant species and highly realistic insects.

The Blessed Virgin's pinnacle

From the shadows, sheltered within a niche, the figure of the Immaculate Conception dominates the pinnacle that tops the Faith portico, loaded with elements of great symbolic content.

⊙ Joseph's anagram
Situated below the Blessed Virgin, the symbol of the Patron of the Catholic Church tops the niche that covers the Presentation of Jesus in the Temple.

Over a three-pointed lamp
The portrayal of the Immaculate Conception, the Catholic dogma according to which Mary was born free of the original sin in order to bear the Son of God, is depicted in a traditional pose in Christian iconography, with her arms crossed upon her chest, and supported by an enormous three-pointed lamp, symbol of the Holy Trinity, which lights up the world thanks to its three candles. Around the niche that holds the Immaculate Conception, Gaudí had bunches of grapes and ears of wheat sculpted, which symbolise the Eucharist, whilst above the image of the Virgin Mary, where the portal culminates, he proposed carving the enigmatic representation of Divine Providence: an eye that opens on the palm of an outstretched hand and which represents the capacity of God to foresee and direct the destiny of the world and humankind.

54 METRES
high is the pinnacle of the Blessed Virgin, the culmination of the Faith portico.

Three-pointed lamp
The carving of the Virgin settles over this symbol of the Trinity.

⊙ The Virgin Mary
Llorenç Matamala, responsible for the temple's team of sculptors, is the creator of this work.

Vine leaves

Ears of wheat

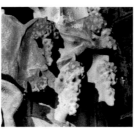
Bunches of grapes

Divine Providence

08 | SACRIFICE AND DEATH SCULPTED IN STONE
The Passion façade

Gaudí's project, materialized by Catalan sculptor Josep Maria Subirachs, reflects Jesus' suffering.

When developing the general project of the basilica, Antoni Gaudí decided to dedicate the temple's three façades to the most transcendental moments of Jesus' life: the Nativity, the Passion and the Glory. During this period, in the early 1890's, Gaudí was already planning to provide the Passion façade with a rather sinister air and believed that if he started off his iconographic project with this portal it might prove to be counterproductive, which subsequently led him to believe that the Nativity, the festive façade, ought to be constructed first. Two decades on, in the year 1911, with the Nativity façade still unfinished, the architect fell ill with Maltese fever and had to move to the Pyrenean town of Puigcerdà whose cleaner air would help him to recuperate more quickly than if he were in industrialised Barcelona. During his forced convalescence, Gaudí came close to death –he even drew up a will–, and this inspired him to finish off the façade that was to relate the final days of Jesus' life; he did it immersed in this spirit of anguish and later acknowledged that he wanted this façade to scare its viewers. The result were the sketches that served as inspiration in order that construction work on the temple was taken up again in 1954 on this façade, despite Gaudí having only outlined its decorative details, leaving future generations with the task of interpreting the sculptural program. This labour was taken on, in the year 1986 –once the structure of the portico and the four bell towers were completed–, by sculptor Josep Maria Subirachs, who took care to capture all the pain and sorrow that Gaudí had envisaged for this façade which is oriented, packed with symbolism, towards the sunset.

Six tilting columns
Inspired by sequoia trunks, they support the portico that holds the twelve sculptural groups on the Passion façade.

The sculptures
The abstraction and angled features typical of Subirachs' work convey the sadness of the Passion of Jesus Christ.

Simon of Cyrene and Three Marys

The representation of pain

The first sector of the temple that was completely carried out in the presence of architect Antoni Gaudí, the Passion façade depicts the cruelty of Jesus' final hours by means of twelve sculptural groups.

3
The Flagellation
Situated in front of the Gospel portal, this sculpture shows the martyrdom of Jesus before being crucified.

Decorative austerity

Antoni Gaudí devised the Passion façade to be stark and restrained in order to convey the severity of the sacrifice of Jesus. On the naked lines of the walls twelve sculptural groups stand out whose purpose is to explain the hours that passed between the Last Supper and the Resurrection of Jesus Christ, in a sequence that freely interprets the Stations of the Cross –the Pathway to Calvary– that is chronologically developed creating a large 'S' on the façade. In front of the wall, six tilted columns increase the sensation of nudity. Their grooves reach out without ornamental interruptions conjuring up enormous sequoias that support a roof over which Gaudí planned a pediment that was composed of 18 bone-like pillars.

✱
THE SCULPTURES

1. The Last Supper
2. Peter and the soldiers and The Kiss of Judas
3. The Flagellation
4. The Denial of Peter
5. Ecce Homo and The Trial of Jesus
6. The Three Marys and Simon of Cyrene
7. The Veronica and the Evangelist
8. Saint Longinus
9. Soldiers playing dice
10. The Crucifixion
11. The Torn Veil
12. The Burial

13
Conventicles
Symbolise the conspirations against Jesus.

Pediment that crowns the façade

Slate cornice

Tilted columns

First sketch carried out by Gaudí

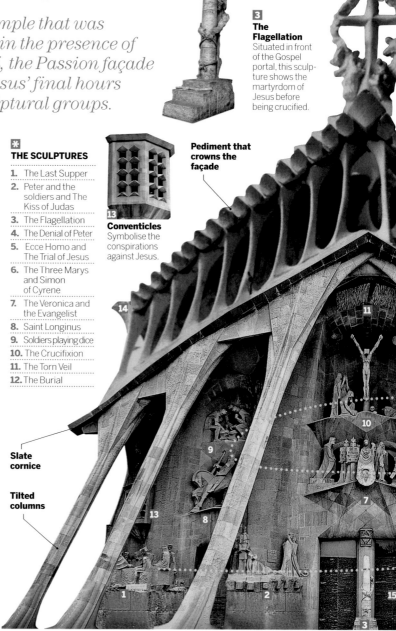

❝ ANTONI GAUDÍ

It is possible that someone finds this façade too extravagant, but I wanted it to frighten, and to achieve this I will not cut back on the chiaroscuro...”

1954

IS THE YEAR
in which the building of the structure of the Passion façade is begun, starting up in this way construction work on the basilica.

Iesus Nazarenus, Rex Iudaeorum
INRI, the anagram that the Romans put on Christ's cross.

The dove
The representation of the Holy Spirit is located above the portal.

The Ascension
The façade is crowned by the sculpture of Jesus in heaven.

Original drawing of the façade, carried out by Gaudí in 1911

40

METRES
is the height that the enormous cross reaches that crowns the pediment on the Passion façade.

Columns
Symbols of death, 18 bones hold up the façade pediment.

The Gospel doors

Sandstone columns

The lion and the lamb
The pediment is finished at its far ends by statues of two animals symbolising Jesus.

Subirachs' masterpiece

After dedicating one year to the study of Gaudí's work, avant-garde sculptor Josep Maria Subirachs was commissioned with creating twelve sculptural ensembles on the Passion façade from 1987 to 2005. During this time, just like Gaudí did in his final years, Subirachs resided in a modest living area within the basilica so he could dedicate his complete attention to what was going to become the masterpiece of his career.

WORKS. THE EVOLUTION OF THE FAÇADE

1960
Foundations
Work started up again with the foundations of the façade.

1965
The portals
They are erected several metres from the façade walls.

1969
The portico
Below the scaffolding the portico structure can be made out.

Biblical characters
Over the cornice that tops the roof of the portico the names of patriarchs and prophets can be read.

The Apostles in the Last Supper
In this group, Subirachs manages to express the desolation of Jesus' disciples by providing them with very schematic faces.

Jesus' last night

On the lower level of the Passion façade, Josep Maria Subirachs depicts with his angled and schematic sculptures the facts concerning the Last Supper and the Betrayal by Judas in Gethsemane.

◉ **Saint John the Apostle**
The youngest of the apostles and Jesus' favourite disciple expresses total grief before the omens of the Messiah, resting his head on his arms.

Tension and sorrow

In the chronological account of the Passion of Jesus represented on the portico, the first sculptural group is the one situated on the lower left-hand side, which reproduces the Last Supper. On it, the gaunt and abstract faces of the Messiah and his apostles, so characteristic of Subirach's style, convey the affliction and grief of the moment in which Jesus, with his back turned, in the centre of the composition, explains to his disciples the facts about to take place, whilst Judas, at one side, secretly clasps the betrayal money. To the right, between the Gethsemane and the Gospel doorways, the narrative thread of The Passion continues with the scene in which Peter faces the soldiers and the moment in which Judas kisses Jesus to indicate whom they have to arrest, a sculpture in which the artist manages to convey the tense atmosphere.

✳ **The Last Supper**
Subirachs opted for an unprecedented composition in the history of art when depicting this scene, with Jesus' back to the viewer and the disciples in a semi-circle.

Judas Iscariot
The apostle that betrayed Jesus is sat on the far right-hand side of the Last Supper group.

Apostle Saint Peter

Bartholomew, Thomas, Philip

Judas Thaddaeus

ART. THE LAST SUPPER OF JESUS AND THE APOSTLES

Throughout the ages numerous artists have depicted this fact from The New Testament, amongst them Renaissance painter Juan de Juanes, in a work carried out around 1562.

'The Last Supper', by Juan de Juanes

10.5

METRES
is the length of the Last Supper sculptural arrangement, devised and carved by sculptor Josep Maria Subirachs based on Gaudí's global idea and comprised of thirteen figures: Jesus and his 12 apostles.

The dog. At Judas' feet, it symbolises loyalty.

1
Malchus' ear
Subirachs reproduces the High Priest's servant's ear that Peter cut off.

2
Mark, 14:45
It is the verse of the Gospel that narrates the betrayal of Judas.

Matthew and Simon

James the Lesser

Jesus explains to his apostles what will happen

310
DIFFERENT COMBINATIONS
of the numbers of the cryptogram always add up to 33, the age Christ died.

Peter and the soldiers. In the scene, the Apostle Peter tries to stop the soldiers from taking Jesus prisoner and in the scuffle he cuts off the high priest's servant's ear.

The magic square
Of great tradition in Muslim culture and in the Jewish Cabbala, the so-called magic squares highlight the symbolism of a specific number, in this case thirty-three.

Jesus Christ

*
The kiss of betrayal
Completing his strategy, Judas kisses Jesus in order to indicate to the soldiers who they should arrest.

Judas
Subirachs does not sculpt the figures of this group in a very defined way as a reminder that the betrayal took place at night.

The robe
The curve of the creases contrasts with the rigidity of Jesus.

The symbol of Judas' betrayal
Present in the sculptural group of the Kiss of Judas, the serpent –a reptile that represents terrestrial imperfection and the lower passions– symbolises the presence of the devil and evil in the apostle's betrayal.

The Flagellation

The scene that depicts Jesus' martyr-dom is on the lower level of the façade in line with the vertical axis that unites this group with the Crucifixion and the Ascension of the Messiah.

The column of Jesus' solitude

Subirachs gave a special relevance to one of the stations of the Way of the Cross –the Flagellation of Christ– providing it with a sculptural group separate from the wall and in a prime position, opposite the door's mullion, at the same height of all those who enter and leave the temple. Carved in travertine, the flagellation shows Jesus alone and dejected, tied to a column, after being tortured by the legionnaires. The sculptor put this group in the centre of the façade, forming a narrative unit with the sculptures of the Crucifixion –high up in the portico– and the Ascension, on the bridge joining the two central towers. The three steps over which the column rises symbolise the days that passed between the Crucifixion and the Resurrection.

✳
The Flagellation
Five metres high, this group is placed, symboli-cally, between Judas, Jesus' betrayer, and Peter, who denied know-ing him three times.

The fossil
According to Subirachs, on the travertine a palm leaf fossil was found, sym-bol of martyrdom.

The Flagellation cane

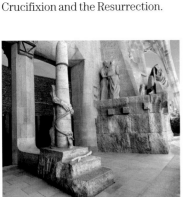

The Flagellation and the Gospel Door

The Column of Martyrdom

1.80 m

5 m

1987
IS THE YEAR
in which the sculptural group of the Flagella-tion is put into place in its space opposite the Gospel Door.

The knot
Sculpted with great realism, it symbolises the physical torture that Jesus underwent.

The column
Divided into four cylinders that symbol-ise the four arms of the cross, the col-umn is out of joint or dis-torted in order to rep-resent the end of the ancient world.

Travertine
The material that Subirachs chose is the same as the construc-tions of Ancient Rome.

The denial and the trial

The lower level of the façade is completed, on either sides of the Coronation of Thorns door, with the groups of Apostle Saint Peter's denial, the Ecce Homo and Jesus' trial before the Roman governor Pontius Pilate.

The Roman eagle
It tops a column on which is written "Tiberius, Emperor of Rome", which historically situates the Passion of Christ.

The Ecce Homo and the trial
The group is divided into two scenes: the first, Pilate presents Jesus to the people, and in the second washes his hands.

1
The cockerel
It forms part of the group of the Denial of Peter.

2
The labyrinth
Borrowed from medieval cathedrals, it evokes Jesus' *Viacrucis.*

Peter's denial
The three women symbolise the three times that Peter denied knowing Jesus. The apostle is upset by his own cowardice.

The doors

For the execution of the two side doors and the large central entrance of the Passion façade, the sculptor decided to use bronze, a material that allowed him to work the shape and textures in great detail.

◉
Alpha and omega
Situated over the mullion of the Gospel Doorway, the first and the last letter of the Greek alphabet represent the beginning and the end, and symbolise God and Christ.

The Gospel Door

Gaudí devised three doors for the façade: the Gospel one, in the centre; the Gethsemane one, to the left, and the Coronation of Thorns, to the right. The central entrance is situated behind the Flagellation and it is divided into two doors measuring almost six metres high that explain, with raised lettering, what the sculptures of the façade express in stone: the Gospel texts relating to Jesus' last two days. The Gethsemane Door illustrates by means of embossed letters Jesus' prayers in the garden and the weakness of the disciples that accompanied him, while the Coronation of Thorns door holds a relief on the upper section that represents the humiliation that the soldiers inflicted on Jesus after torturing him and, in the central section, the scenes of the Presentation of the Messiah before Herod and Pontius Pilate.

Letters and images in relief
The most relevant words are polished in order that they stand out from the oxide.

Raised letters
The imposing Gospel doors function like the pages of a monumental New Testament bible.

8,000
DIFFERENT CHARACTERS
are cast to make up the texts that appear on the doors.

RELIEFS. GRAPHIC SYMBOLS

Amongst words and phrases that narrate the Passion of Christ on the doors of the façade, Subirachs inserted numerous related graphic symbols, of very different sizes, like the cryptogram that is repeated on the wall or Gaudí's signature, a homage to the temple's architect.

Magic square

Jesus in Gethsemane

Gaudí's signature

Maltese Cross

The Coronation of Thorns door

Polished bronze face

The Gethsemane door. Phrases and signs are combined on it with large-size sculptural bas-reliefs.

4.41
METRES
high is the Gethsemane door, on the Passion façade.

The full moon
Image of night and harbinger of death.

Melancholy
Shape inspired by a work from the painter Albrecht Dürer.

2000
IS THE YEAR
in which the Coronation of Thorns door is put into place in the basilica.

'The Divine Comedy'
The Coronation doorway includes a quote from a poem.

1

The Coronation
A soldier ridicules Christ giving a cane as a sceptre after crowning him with thorns.

1

Cast bronze

The Coronation of Thorns door. It's five metres high and is comprised of a fixed piece and two hinged doors.

To the crucifixion

The intermediate section of the Passion façade relates in three sculptural groups the most relevant facts about the route that Jesus Christ followed laden with the cross up to Mount Calvary, where he was crucified.

1 The Veronica
The episode of the meeting of Jesus with the Veronica does not appear in the canonical Gospels. This is one of the reasons that the carving lacks a face.

Veronica's veil

Situated over the Gospel door, the central sculptural arrangement of the intermediate level symbolizes Veronica's veil, a scene that narrates the second fall of Jesus on the Way of the Cross and the meeting with the women of Jerusalem, one of whom –Veronica– wipes blood off Jesus' face with a cloth or veil and is left with an image of the Messiah imprinted on it. Carved in bas-relief, Jesus' face always seems to be looking at the observer, no matter where the latter's location; the figure of Veronica, in contrast, lacks features, in order to symbolically reinforce the face of the Messiah stamped on the cloth. The legionaries that accompany the scene, inspired by the chimneys of La Pedrera, are a homage by Subirachs to Gaudí.

✳ To the crucifixion
The scene for the Road to Calvary occupies the central part and is found on the same line as the Flagellation and the group of the Death of Jesus.

17 FIGURES
make up the sculptural arrangement that comprises Veronica's Veil.

The Evangelist
Subirachs used a photo of Gaudí to depict him as the evangelist that tells the facts.

Jesus' second fall on the way
In the same sculptural group of the Veronica, Subirachs depicts the fall of the Messiah before the women of Jerusalem and the Evangelist.

3 The face of Jesus Christ
Subirachs uses the bas-relief technique, which he was an expert on, in order to effectively reproduce the face of Jesus printed on the cloth.

The women of Jerusalem
This scene evokes Jesus' words to the women: "Daughters of Jerusalem, stop weeping for Me; but weep for yourselves and for your children".

➡ **Simon of Cyrene and Three Marys**
This sculptural group is a representation of Jesus' third fall.

⬅ **Suffering**
The faces express Jesus' pain as well as the witnesses.

Spectators
Subirachs reproduces the people of the city.

Jesus fallen
The sculpture conveys Christ's suffering.

4

2

1990

IS THE YEAR
the Pathway to Calvary and the Veronica arrangement are put into place –works by Josep Maria Subirachs– on the Passion façade.

Sculpted sandstone cross

Longinus and Simon de Cyrene

The groups that flank the Veronica group represent Longinus, the soldier that pierced Jesus in his side with his lance –converted later to Christianity and canonized a Saint by the Church–, and the scene of the Three Marys and Simon of Cyrene, who assists a faint Jesus to carry the cross to Mount Calvary.

✳ **Longinus**
The soldier pierces the façade with his lance.

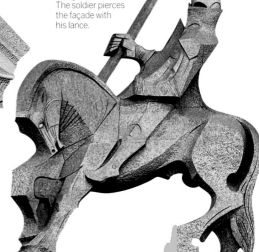

REFERENCES. HOMAGES TO GAUDÍ

Subirachs recalls the architect on several places of the façade: the evangelist in the Veronica group looks like him, the chimneys of Casa Milà are evoked and Gaudí's signature is reproduced on a door.

5

Antoni Gaudí

6

La Pedrera

The Death of Jesus

The upper level is presided over by the figure of Jesus Christ crucified, the culminating scene of the Passion façade, surrounded by the group of soldiers playing for the Messiah's apparel and the burial group.

Mary Magdalene at the feet of Christ
The figure is on its knees below the cross, at the feet of Jesus Christ crucified, attached to the edge of the architectonic plinth of the façade.

Jesus Christ crucified

In the Crucifixion group, Jesus is tied to a cross composed of two iron beams, one of whose profiles are painted in red to highlight the 'I' of INRI, initials from the Latin inscription "Jesus of Nazareth, King of the Jews" that the Romans put over the cross. At the feet of the Messiah, is Mary Magdalene, kneeling, Mary of Clopas and the Virgin, with her face covered and consoled by Saint John. At the base of the cross, a skull symbolises death and the name of the place where Christ was crucified –*Gólgota* means 'cranium' in Aramaic–, while the open tomb presages the Resurrection. To the left of the group, Subirachs represented the scene of the soldiers that share out the apparel of the condemned man, and to the right, the burial of Christ, composed as an immense Pieta, in which Mary, Joseph of Arimathea and Nicodemus deposit Jesus' body in the tomb.

Soldier playing for Jesus' robes

1

5
METRES
is the height of the sculpture of Christ crucified that presides over The Passion.

Knucklebones
The table where the soldiers play is inspired by the bones they used to bet with.

1
The legionnaires
Gambing was a pastime that proved popular amongst Roman soldiers.

The initial 'I' of acronym INRI

The face of Jesus crucified

The Virgin Mary

Mary of Clopas

↩ The Crucifixion
Subirachs concentrates all the characters of the scene to the left of the composition and puts the symbols to the right.

Death
The skull at the foot of the cross represents death and the name of the place where Christ was crucified.

30×30
CENTIMETRES
is the thickness of the beams that form the cross that supports Christ's figure.

The moon
The gospels narrate that when Jesus Christ died night fell upon Jerusalem.

Easter egg, resurrection symbol

✳ The burial
The last group of the façade stages the burial of Jesus in the Holy Sepulchre.

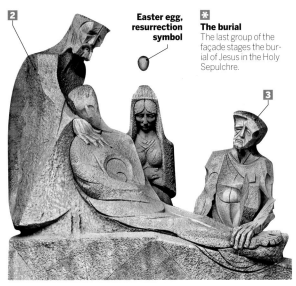

Joseph of Arimathea

Nicodemus

01

02

03

04

01 to 03
Detail of
the atrium
The vault that covers the portico is covered with a series of inscriptions, letters and drawings carried out in Venetian glasswork. One of them, the lamb, symbolises Jesus Christ's resurrection.

04
The torn cloth
As if it were an enormous baldachino over the cross, this bronze structure covers the scene of the death of the Messiah, depicting the curtain inside the Temple of Jerusalem that separated the central zone from the other holier areas. According to the Gospel, this curtain split into two pieces at the very moment that Jesus died, permitting the view of the upper arch of the atrium.

05
The Ascension
of Christ
Carried out in bronze by Subirachs and weighing around two tonnes, this monumental sculpture hangs from the bridge that joins the towers of Bartholomew and Thomas, over the Passion façade.

09 | THE BASILICA'S MOST IMPORTANT FAÇADE
The Glory façade

Gaudí dedicates the façade to the glorification of Jesus Christ and to the pathway of Man to reach eternal life.

With the aim of leaving something behind for his successors to refer to, in 1916 –ten years before his death– the architect carried out an indepth study of the constructive structure and the symbolic plan that the Glory façade should have. In order to support his decisions, as was his custom, he had a model made up to demonstrate total volume and on which the ideas he had devised for the basilica's largest façade could be seen applied. However, this model –the best guide that architects posterior to Gaudí could have counted on in order to carry out the façade– was destroyed in the year 1936, by the fire in the temple's workshop during the uprising at the start of the Civil War. Nowadays, this study model can be found partially reconstructed, but the most significant legacy for the construction of this façade have been the photographs and accounts left by the selfsame architect and his collaborators. Nonetheless, one of the aspects where there is much more documentation is that which is related to the urban development project of the temple's surroundings and, above all, what corresponds to the Glory façade that Antoni Gaudí left for implementation. The project devises a large platform followed by a vast flight of steps that overcomes the more than five metre drop between the naves –that of the main floor– and the road. On this platform the architect puts two large monuments –dedicated to water and fire– and underneath devises a tunnel which the traffic will pass through on Mallorca Street. However, one of the most important aspects is the landscaped esplanade that runs in front of the temple with the objective of obtaining a better view of the Glory façade and the entire arrangement.

Gaudí's model of the façade
The twisted metal filaments over the lanterns simulate the clouds that the architect imagined for decorating the façade.

Ornamentation and symbology
The main entrance to the temple is accessed by seven bronze doors carried out by Subirachs.

Mystery of the Faith

Water jug

The temple's main façade

Orientated towards the midday sun the Glory façade is the largest and most monumental of the basilica, with a structure formed by large lanterns of different height and size as its main distinguishing feature.

The lanterns and clouds

The Glory façade is the monumental framework Gaudí devised to provide entry to the temple. His idea was that, before entering the holy enclosure, worshippers would be conscious of the role of man inside the general order of Creation and of his destiny in accordance with the Divine laws: Death, the Final Judgement, Hell and Glory. Below the apostles' towers such as Saint Peter's, Saint Paul's, Saint Andrew's and James the Elder's –higher than those that top the other façades–, the architect designed an ensemble of 16 unequal lanterns of hyperboloid layout, one of which –the central one– rises until it competes with the towers. Over this structure, which serves as a roof for the portico, Gaudí envisaged a cluster of large, illuminated clouds containing the words from the Creed, the prayer that resumes the dogma of Christian faith.

Illuminated clouds

4

➐ Gaudí's model
It reproduces in plaster the shapes devised by the architect for the Glory façade.

16 LANTERNS
make up the portico's roof that provides access to the temple.

Saint Andrew's bell tower

➜ **Berenguer's interpretation**
Gaudí's collaborator carried out this polychrome illustration that was inspired by the original plan devised by the architect.

2002
IS THE YEAR
in which construction work on the Glory façade gets off to a start.

1
Jesus
The resurrected Messiah's image is in the centre of the façade, below the decorative top.

Baptistery
Free-standing building, situated to the left of the façade.

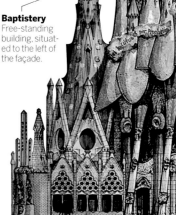

LANTERNS. INSPIRATION

The configuration of the lanterns, generated via revolving hyperboloids, is inspired by the alternation of rounded and sharp shapes from the massif of Montserrat, where the Patron Saint of Catalonia is worshipped.

Gaudí's models

Massif of Montserrat

> **ANTONI GAUDÍ**
> "Originality mustn't be searched for, as then it is extravagance. One must observe what is usually done and then try to improve on it"

2
The Creed
The letters over the clouds are illuminated so they can be read from far away.

20
METRES
high reaches the water from the fountain monument on the esplanade.

3
Columns
Fifteen sturdy columns hold up the roof of the portico of the façade.

4
Narration of Genesis

Gaudí's ideas. Five blocks of unbuilt on, gardened areas will make up a Latin cross around the basilica once finished.

The 1975 urban development plan
The proposal for the development and landscaping of surroundings.

The basilica and the city
According to Gaudí's project, access to the Glory portico is carried out by means of a flight of steps followed by an esplanade where monuments related to fire and water are located. Below this platform is the tunnel which traffic on Mallorca Street goes through, while at the bottom of the steps, and up to Diagonal Avenue, a garden stretches out offering a much broader perspective of the main façade.

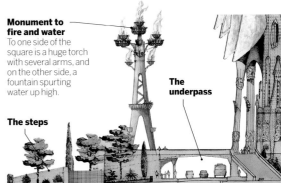

Monument to fire and water
To one side of the square is a huge torch with several arms, and on the other side, a fountain spurting water up high.

The steps

The underpass

The Glory façade portal

As a symbol of the pillars of the Christian faith, seven tilted columns and eight vertical ones support the portico which worshippers go through into the temple, crossing the seven doors dedicated to the sacraments.

The tilted columns
Just like on the Passion façade, Antoni Gaudí proposed using tilted columns in order to improve the support that the Glory portico received.

Fifteen columns and seven doors

The portico that precedes access to the temple forms a wide atrium covered by hyperboloid vaults and supported by two rows of columns: seven ones tilting outwardly in the foreground with eight vertical ones in the background. Each one of the exterior columns has the name engraved of one of the seven gifts from the Holy Spirit, while on the bases appear the seven capital sins, and on the capitals, the opposing virtues. Half hidden amongst the interior columns are the seven doors accessing the naves, dedicated to the sacraments of the church and to a petition of The Lord's Prayer. Each one of the portico's doors connects with one of the naves of the temple, except for the main central one, which is divided into three openings.

The seven doors
They are installed at different depths due to the undulations that were designed in the wall.

Study model
It is inspired by the scale model that Gaudí had carried out to illustrate his ideas.

2012
IS THE YEAR
in which the central doors of the Glory façade are hung into place.

The windows
The reinforced concrete structure that supports the façade incorporates large glass windows —which evolve along the façade— in order to illuminate the inside of the basilica.

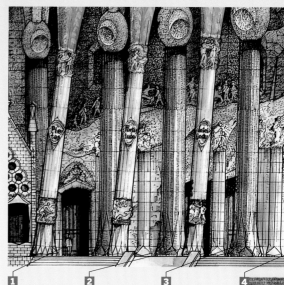

1 Baptism door
The first sacrament is represented by the start of the prayer.

2 The Extreme Unction door
The phrase "Thy Kingdom come" is used for this sacrament.

3 The door of Order
The line "Thy will be done on Earth as it is in Heaven" is quoted.

4

Depictions of biblical scenes

On the façade there are different chapters from the Old and New Testament that are reproduced by means of sculptural groups related to the evolution of humanity from the Creation up until the Resurrection.

Adam and Eve

Noah's Ark

Final Judgement

Glory or Heaven

Hell

2,000
KILOS
is the weight of each one of the bronze doors of the Eucharist door.

Eucharist symbol
Over the Eucharist door there is the image of a chalice.

The portico
Hyperboloid vaults lit up by the lanterns cover the façade's portico.

50
IS THE NUMBER
of different languages in which the Lord's Prayer can be read on the Glory façade's Eucharist door.

4
The Eucharist door
The central portal providing access into the temple reproduces all of the Lord's Prayer.

5
Confirmation door
"Forgive us our trespasses as we forgive those who trespass against us".

6
Matrimony door
The phrase, "Lead us not into temptation", is employed.

7
Penitence door
"And deliver us from evil" is the phrase culminating the prayer.

Hell, judgement and paradise

According to the symbolic program devised by Gaudí, the Glory façade reproduced the path taken by Man to reach eternal life. Accustomed to combining the functional and ornamental, the architect makes the most of the semi-darkness of the underpass below the steps to represent hell by means of closed windows with bars –in order to convey that nobody can free themselves from sin without faith– and sculptures of tombs and demonic creatures. On the surface, over the doors, are Adam and Eve, the protagonists of Creation and parents of the human race, while the highest area of the central focal point is reserved for the Virgin, whose gaze is on Jesus, who seems to be judging Humanity. A large rose window symbolises the Holy Spirit and above it, on the highest point of the arrangement, is the majestic figure of God the Father.

> **ANTONI GAUDÍ**
>
> **The building of the Sagrada Familia is slow, because the master of this work is in no hurry"**

The Eucharist door. Work of sculptor Josep Maria Subirachs, who is also author of the sculptural program of the Passion façade, the doors on the Glory façade's main entrance respond to Gaudí's express wish that the Lord's Prayer appear –in words and image– on the Glory portico. In accordance with the ideas of the temple's architect, Subirachs reproduced all the petitions from the mentioned prayer using large size letters in Catalan on a surface formed by a texture of the same Lord's prayer in forty-nine other languages, written in smaller letters.

10

THE RECUPERATION OF THE GOTHIC SPIRIT

The bell towers and the cimborios

The basilica was planned to be the highest construction in the city and to bring the work closer to God.

In any period or civilization religious constructions have stood apart for their monumentality and dimensions, and in particular for their height, a quality that bestows prestige and dignity on a building and is, in itself, a mystic symbol, given that it represents the union between heaven and earth. In the Middle Ages, revolutionary Gothic architects managed to build much higher buildings than their predecessors thanks, principally, to the invention of the ogival arch and the cross vault, which managed to lighten the walls and roofs of the temples and, in consequence, meant that cathedrals could reach heights that had been unimaginable until that time. Centuries later, imbued by the same spirit that fired these medieval architects, Antoni Gaudí wanted to convert the Basilica of the Sagrada Familia into the highest construction in Barcelona. With this objective he designed

Jesus' tower –the culmination of the temple– to be 172.5 metres high, a measurement that would make it the tallest religious building in the world, but would leave it just a few metres below Montjuïc, the highest hill in the municipality of Barcelona in the late nineteenth century, when building work on the basilica commenced. With this decision, Gaudí showed a great desire to construct a building that would urbanistically mark the city while at the same time venerate and respect God's work – Montjuïc–, which in his opinion Man should never try to exceed. Finally, out of the eighteen towers of the arrangement –the six cimborios dedicated to Jesus, Mary and the Evangelists and the twelve bell towers representing the Apostles– he only got to see one complete: Barnabus' bell tower, finished in 1925, a few months prior to his death.

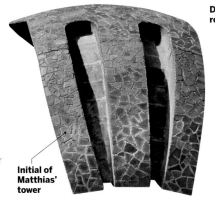

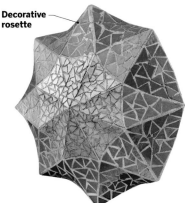

⬅ The Nativity bell towers
Of parabolic profile, the pinnacles of the towers of the eastern façade rise 100 metres above street level.

➡ The glazed *trencadís* mosaic
The spires of the towers are visible from far away thanks to the Venetian *trencadís* cladding.

Initial of Matthias' tower

Decorative rosette

The culmination of the basilica

*Gaudí planned a temple of great verti-
cality in order that it could be visible
from any point in Barcelona with
18 towers from 98 to 172 metres that
rose above the buildings of the city.*

Cimborios and bell towers

Gaudí devised the elevations of the
18 towers of the Sagrada Familia in
order that they grow in height according to the symbolic hierarchy of
whom they represent and in accordance with their position in relation to
the centre of the temple's ground
plan: Jesus' cimborio culminates the
ensemble at 172.5 metre high and is
seated over the crossing. The four
Evangelist cimborios reach 135 metres and rise up flanking the largest
cimborio, as well as the Virgin Mary
one, which rises 130 metres over the
apse. Finally, the twelve bell towers,
dedicated to the apostles, rise, in
groups of four, on the periphery of
the building, over the three porticos
providing access, and measure from
98 to 120 metres. In order to get the
most out of the visual and symbolic
aspect, all the towers culminate in
spires clad in glazed ceramic work
from the Island of Murano (Italy).

1
**JESUS'
CIMBORIO**

172.5
METRES
is the height of the
most important tower
of the basilica
designed by Gaudí.

2
**MARY'S
CIMBORIO**

130
METRES
is the height reached
by the tower dedicat-
ed to the Virgin,
topped by a star.

Nativity bell towers
Dedicated to Barna-
bus, Matthias, Simon
and Judas.

Cloister

⊖
**Termination
of the pinnacles
of the bell towers**
They represent the
symbols that distin-
guish bishops.

✱ Models of tower
Gaudí designed
four types of tow-
er: the bell towers,
the Evangelists'
cimborios, the Vir-
gin Mary's tower
and Jesus' tower.

**Four-armed
cross**

**Termination of
Saint John the
Evangelist's
cimborio**

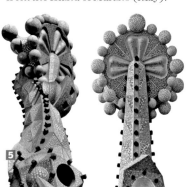

General project

Nativity façade

Passion façade

INFLUENCES
The inspiration

The singular parabolic profile of the bell towers have been associated to different influences, result of Gaudí's intuitive capacity for observation.

3 THE EVANGELIST CIMBORIOS

135
METRES
is the total height reached by each one of the towers dedicated to the Evangelists.

4 THE APOSTLE BELL TOWERS

120
METRES
is the maximum height of the bell towers, while the minimum is 98 metres.

Bell towers on the Passion side
They are dedicated to Thomas, James the Lesser, Bartholomew and Philip, Jesus' apostles.

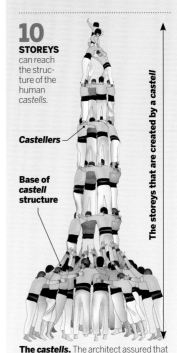

10
STOREYS
can reach the structure of the human *castells.*

Castellers

Base of *castell* structure

The storeys that are created by a castell

The *castells*. The architect assured that the bell towers and the cimborios of the temple obeyed the same law of balance as the human towers of Catalonia.

The temple. The towers dominate the urban landscape.

Inside the bell towers
Inside the upper part the basilica's bells are located.

> ANTONI
> **GAUDÍ**
> **The towers' shape, vertical and parabolic, is the union of gravity with light... On the highest part will be bright lights, like natural light that comes from the sky"**

6

Valley of the Fairies, Turkey
These natural forms are found in Capadocia.

African mosques
Antoni Gaudí saw them when he made a trip to Morocco.

The bell towers

Dedicated to the twelve apostles, the Sagrada Familia's bell towers make up the background canvas of the Nativity, Passion and Glory façades, and configure the more characteristic profiles of the construction.

Apostle Saint Judas Thaddeus

The mitre of the bishops

From Earth to Heaven

Provided with an innovative parabolic design, the bell towers designed by Gaudí start off with a squared base and around a quarter of the way up undergo a rapid transition transforming into a circular layout that culminates in their characteristic needle-like shape, result of the application of doubly ruled surfaces, a common resource used by the architect in order that he could imitate structures that he observed in nature. The artist proposed this change of ground plan in order to symbolise by means of the towers the path of the tangible or earthly –represented by the square base– to the celestial, a state that materializes in the formal perfection of the circle. Likewise, Gaudí made the most of this structural transformation in order to support on one of the resulting edges the apostle sculpture to whom each bell tower is dedicated.

The interior. Gaudí put winding staircases in the first part of the façades' bell towers, up to the height of the balconies.

2
Vents for directing sound
Tilted in a downward direction, bell chime sound is directed down to the street.

3
Stars
They decorate the walls of the bell towers, around the praises "Sanctus".

426
STEPS
make up the winding staircases of the Sagrada Familia temple's bell towers.

The Sagrada Familia

4
Prayers on the wall

5
Balconies

6
Bridge between towers

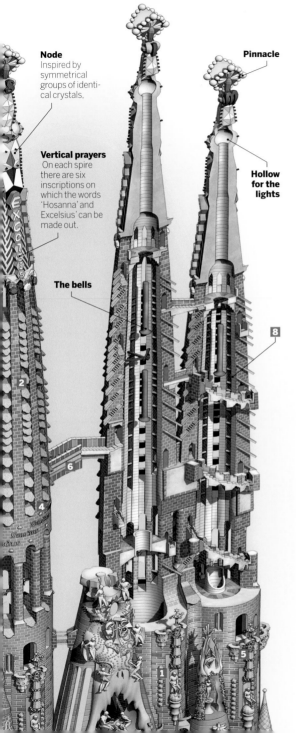

Node
Inspired by symmetrical groups of identical crystals,

Pinnacle

Vertical prayers
On each spire there are six inscriptions on which the words 'Hosanna' and 'Excelsius' can be made out.

Hollow for the lights

The bells

7

7

8

8

1925

IS THE YEAR
the Barnabus tower is finished, the temple's first finished bell tower.

7
Winding staircases
Their attractive shape is inspired by a type of seasnail shell.

8
Space for the bells
They hang in the towers' upper section.

Optimum sound

The interior of Sagrada Familia's bell towers is designed to provide acoustics of the highest quality. Antoni Gaudí had some slightly tilted vents installed in the openings, in order that the sound from the bells could clearly reach the street. To the good sound also contributes the simplicity of the winding staircases, so narrow that a railing proved unnecessary. Up until the bridge the stairs go up on the inside and from then on they are attached to the exterior wall, given that the central part has to be reserved for the bells.

SOUND. THE BELLS

Gaudí thought about providing the temple with 84 common and tubular bells. The last type reproduce all notes and work by percussion or by injected air.

Bell in the Saint Barnabus tower

Tubular bells

The Nativity façade apostles
They are the first towers to be finished and dedicated to the Apostles Matthias, Barnabus, Simon and Judas Thaddaeus.

The Apostles on the Passion façade
Directed to the west they are dedicated to the Apostles Bartholomew, Philip, Thomas and James the Lesser.

The pinnacles

Gaudí had the terminations of the bell towers made with glazed Venetian ceramic work so that the symbols he designed, identifiable with whom each tower was dedicated to, were visible from far away.

Rosettes
On the base of the pinnacle, at the end of the body of the tower, each bell tower has twelve rosettes attached of various colours, clad, like other elements of the pinnacle, with Venetian ceramic work with the *trencadís* technique.

The endings of the bell towers

Gaudí envisaged complex solutions for the terminations of the twelve Apostles' towers. The first consisted of a look-out tower of hexagonal base and pyramidal shape with rings. The second, which was what was finally carried out, tops each bell tower with a 25 metre high pinnacle adorned with polychrome Venetian ceramic work. The architect made the most of the tiles' glossy reflection to highlight, using the technique he invented –*trencadís* or broken tile cladding–, the symbology assigned to each bell tower: the initial of the Apostle to whom it is dedicated and the elements that distinguish the bishops –continuers of the evangelical work of Jesus' disciples– represented in a schematic way.

White balls
They are inspired by spheres decorating the mitre.

The cross
It culminates the pinnacle and is part of the mitre symbol.

✳ Shapes and colours
The endings of the towers stand out for their lively polychrome in contrast to the natural grey stone of the rest of the bell tower.

Pinnacle node
Inspired by the crystallization of minerals.

3.75
METRES
is the diameter of the crosses that culminate the pinnacles of the bell towers.

Trencadís

⊖ Polyhedral shapes
The complex geometric designs of the spires are the result of the intersection of various polyhedras.

The mitre
The bishops' head-dress is represented by the double-sided face adorned by white spheres.

The staff
The trunk of the pinnacle slightly leans over on its upper part to recreate the shape of the bishop's staff.

The ring
A symbol of the bishops' authority and their loyalty to the Church, the ring is located below the trunk of the pinnacle.

The symbols of the bishops
Episcopal icons predominate in the symbology devised by Antoni Gaudí for the pinnacles. On all of them with the cross, the staff and the rings can be made out, all with very stylized shapes.

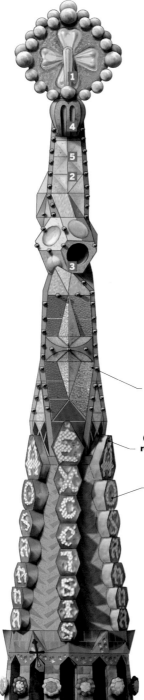

Coloured Venetian work

Glass and reinforced concrete

Prayers on stone

25
METRES
is the total height of the spires that top the bell towers.

1977
IS THE YEAR
The Passion's towers are completed.

The initials of the Apostles
In the narrower part of the pinnacle, just below the cross that culminates all the bell towers, Antoni Gaudí had the initial of Jesus Christ's disciple depicted on each tower. With a convex surface area in order to better reflect the sunlight, these letters are clad with the architect's well-known red, glossy *trencadís* work.

CRAFTWORK. MURANO GLASS

To clad the spires, Gaudí chose Venetian mosaic work, that comes from the Island of Murano and is characterized by the quality of the glass from which it is made.

Venetian mosaic work

Glass pieces

The cimborios

The central part of the roof of the Basilica of the Sagrada Familia is taken up by six cimborios that are the highest elements of the basilica and are dedicated to Jesus Christ, the Virgin Mary and the four Evangelists.

The coronation of the temple

Gaudí gave a lot of importance to the six cimborios in the general context of the temple, given that they illuminate the altar and crown the building. Owing to their great height, the architect designed them with a wider base than that of the bell towers and with a similar profile to that of the sacristies situated on the corners of the cloister, parting from an octagonal plinth whose sides ascend forming convex parabolas. The largest of the cimborios, Jesus' tower, covers the crossing of the temple with its enormous vault and culminates with a four-armed, 15 metre high cross. The Virgin's tower rises over the apse and is crowned by the morning star –an ancient Marian symbol–, and the cimborios of the Evangelists perch over the four sides of Jesus' tower and culminate with the symbols that represent Matthew, Mark, Luke and John.

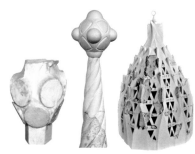

Preliminary studies. Gaudí left behind plaster models of the structures and the different parts of the cimborios.

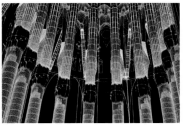

Advanced techniques. Computer technology has been key in order to see the ideas that Gaudí developed for the cimborios materialized.

SYMBOLOGY. THE FOUR-ARMED CROSS

Antoni Gaudí devised this three-dimensional cross to be seen from any view point and he used it throughout his career in many of his projects.

Bellesguard

Park Güell

Casa Batlló

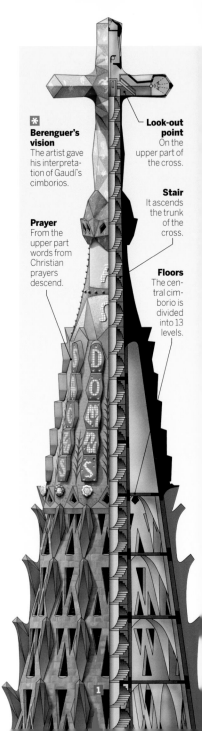

✳ **Berenguer's vision**
The artist gave his interpretation of Gaudí's cimborios.

Prayer
From the upper part words from Christian prayers descend.

Look-out point
On the upper part of the cross.

Stair
It ascends the trunk of the cross.

Floors
The central cimborio is divided into 13 levels.

1

1 Jesus' cimborio

2 Mary's cimborio

3 John the Evangelist's cimborio

Symbol of Saint John

12-pointed star

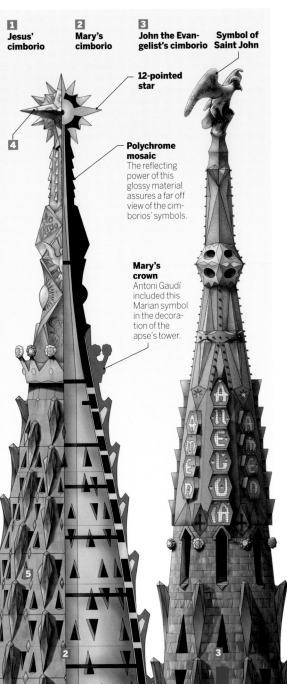

Polychrome mosaic
The reflecting power of this glossy material assures a far off view of the cimborios' symbols.

Mary's crown
Antoni Gaudí included this Marian symbol in the decoration of the apse's tower.

4

Model of Mary's star
The symbol crowning the Virgin's tower is the *Stella Matutina*, a 12-pointed star that directs the Church towards Christ.

5

Decoration of Mary's tower
The cimborio dedicated to the Virgin is covered with a polychrome mosaic of blues, pinks and golds.

15
METRES
high is the cross that crowns Jesus' cimborio, the culminating point of the Basilica of the Sagrada Familia, reaching a grand height of 172.5 metres.

The vault of Mary's tower
Situated over the apse of the basilica, the Virgin Mary's cimborio's interior has a ribbed vault.

MATERIALS
The titanium towers

Titanium is the material chosen to finish off the Evangelist's cimborios for its light weight and its metallic sheen that changes colour in different light.

✳
Titanium qualities
It is a metal that is very resistant in outdoor conditions, such as in damp weather.

Stone base
The structure of the cimborios is natural stone.

←
A metal structure
The pieces of titanium make up a framework that ensures resistance to strong gusts of wind.

4.5
GRAMS/CM³
is the density of titanium, less than that of steel (7.8), which makes it lighter.

The decoration of the towers. As well as the *trencadís* cladding of Venetian glazed mosaic work employed on the pinnacles of the bell towers, Gaudí devised numerous decorative elements for the towers of the Basilica of the Sagrada Familia, such as the prayers and inscriptions dedicated to the Holy Trinity and carved in the same natural stone employed on the construction of the walls –visible from far away– or attached small size pieces – only perceptible from the balconies of the towers– which provide variety and originality to the arrangement.

The symbology of the towers

Gaudí wanted to represent with the Basilica of the Sagrada Família's six cimborios and twelve bell towers the pillars of the Catholic faith: Jesus, the Virgin Mary, the four authors of the New Testament and the Apostles.

Connection between Heaven and Earth
An ensemble of bell towers and cimborios Gaudí devised for the basilica symbolises the temple's condition as a nexus between the earthly and the celestial, represented by soaring towers.

1
JESUS
He is the Son of God and the founder of Christianity, symbolised by Gaudí with the highest tower of the temple and in the city, crowned by a cross.

2
MARY
The virginity of the Mother of God is one of the main dogmas of Catholicism. She is represented by the apse tower, crowned by a star.

3
SAINT MATTHEW
Also called Levi in the Holy Scriptures, he was disciple of Jesus Christ and wrote the first gospel. His traditional symbol is an angel.

THE NATIVITY BELL TOWERS

7
Matthias
He took the place of Judas Iscariot.

8
Judas Thaddaeus
He was James the Lesser's brother.

9
Simon Cananeus
Also known as Simon the Zealot.

10
Barnabus
He preached in Cyprus and Turkey.

THE PASSION BELL TOWERS

11
James the Lesser
Stoned to death for his faith in Christ.

12
Bartholomew
He preached in India and Armenia.

18 TOWERS

are those that rise on the Sagrada Familia: the Jesus one (1) over the crossing; Mary's (2) over the apse; the Evangelist's (3 to 6) around the first, and the twelve bell towers (7 to 18), four on each façade.

THE TOWERS

of the Sagrada Familia make up 4 groups, according to their location on the basilica's ground plan.

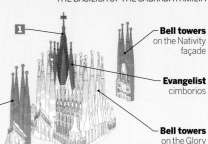

Bell towers on the Nativity façade

Evangelist cimborios

Bell towers on the Passion façade

Bell towers on the Glory façade

4

SAINT MARK

The writer of the second gospel and the first bishop of Alexandria is symbolised by a lion and was interpreter of Saint Peter, father of the Church.

5

SAINT LUKE

The writer of the third gospel is symbolised by an ox. He was companion of the Apostle Saint Paul. Born in Antakya (now Turkey), he wasn't Jewish.

6

SAINT JOHN

Symbolised by the eagle, Saint John is considered one of Jesus's closest apostles and is the author of the Book of the Apocalypse.

THE GLORY BELL TOWERS

13
Thomas
He doubted the Resurrection of Jesus.

14
Philip
He was crucified in Asia Minor.

15
Andrew
He was the first apostle called by Jesus.

16
Peter
Founded the Church and was its first Pope.

17
Paul
He was the first theologist of Christianity.

18
James the Greater
John's brother, he was decapitated.

11 | THE PROVISIONAL CONSTRUCTIONS
The schoolrooms and the workshop

Antoni Gaudí plans buildings of ephemeral nature to provide functions and services to the basilica.

In order to satisfy every necessity related to the construction of such a formidable project such as the Sagrada Familia, Gaudí had to design provisional buildings for the use of workers and their children. One of these functional buildings was the workshop, a construction that encompassed warehouses, studios for artists and craftsmen —where they carried out their works, their sculptures and models— and the architect's own study —where the architect kept the building plans of the temple—. Nonetheless, out of all the annex buildings —the chaplain's residence was another example— those that have undoubtedly aroused the greatest architectonic interest —for their avant-garde structure and aesthetic originality— have been the schoolrooms. The idea of founding a school linked to the Sagrada Familia was thanks to Father Gil Parés i Vilasau, the first chaplain to be custodian of the crypt, who in 1908 proposed that Gaudí construct an inexpensive building that would be used as an education centre for the children of the workers of the temple and for children from modest backgrounds who resided in the neighbourhood. Parés was a keen follower of the educational method of active pedagogy, a very progressive system devised by the Italian Maria Montessori and characterised by its respect for the student as a person, in a period in which corporal punishment was used frequently in the learning process. In order to carry out this project — probably paid for by the architect—, Gaudí had to use all his ingenuity designing a brick building that, despite its structural simplicity and the humbleness of the materials employed, can be included as one of the most representative works of his professional career.

Access to the schoolrooms
Located alongside the basilica, the architect puts a large sign in the main entrance of the area indicating the building's use.

The ground plan
The plan of the building shows the walls' sinuous outlines and the division into three classrooms, with lavatories at the far ends.

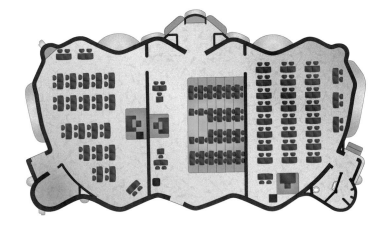

Simple and functional works

The architect shows off all his creative genius, his aesthetic originality and his mastery of constructive solutions in subsidiary buildings whose modest appearance are packed with technical and engineering innovations.

The schoolrooms

With just one floor measuring 24 metres long by 12 metres wide, the building is narrow, with rounded corners, with two partition walls that provide three classrooms and two lavatories at either end. The walls, render-free, are made up of two layers of brick cemented with fast-setting mortar. The constructive technique transgresses traditional methods: the bricks are laid on their larger side –as interior partitions in houses are usually laid– and vertically positioned –in order to make the façade curve more easily–. For the roof, three iron pillars support a master beam of the same material, which runs through the axis of the building and acts as a support to a series of smaller wooden beams, forming a warped roof, light and resistant at the same time.

Magnolia leaf
Gaudí was inspired by the curve of these leaves for the schoolrooms' roof.

1928
IS THE YEAR
Le Corbusier visits the schoolrooms and studies its structure.

The roof
Shaped by a balance of beams over the central girder.

3
Central room
It has direct access to the exterior.

Illumination
Despite the fact that Antoni Gaudí installed windows on all four walls in order to get maximum natural light all day long, he also installed electrical lighting.

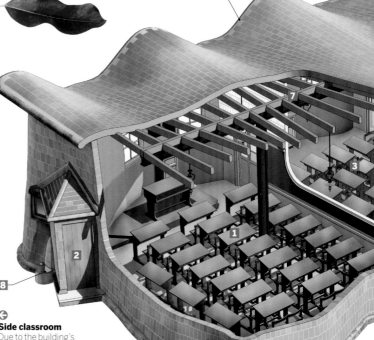

7

3

1

2

8

1

Side classroom
Due to the building's relocation, the schoolrooms' original appearance was recuperated –lost after the 1936 reconstruction– with the help of period furniture.

2
Lavatory entrance

Bricks in *stretcher* and *sailor* style

6
Windows
Finished off with a pediment of obliquely positioned bricks.

7
Ceiling beams
They rest on the walls constituting the singular rolling shape of the roof.

Roof with three layers of brick

Warped surface

150
STUDENTS
were how many pupils could be educated within the schoolrooms' walls.

5

6

Wall with curved surface

Perimetral stone plinth

4
Main entrance
A triangular protrusion on the west wall means the inclusion of a small vestibule is possible, with two doors.

5
Water drainage
The schoolrooms' roof's warped brick surface meant that any rainfall would be instantly and easily disposed of.

8
The schoolrooms' water fountain
Mary's symbol can be seen over the circular stone basin.

9,000
PESETAS
equivalent to fifty-four euros, was the cost of construction of the schoolrooms.

1936
IS THE YEAR
when the schoolrooms caught fire as well as other parts of the temple, two days after the *coup d'état* that was the start of the Spanish Civil War.

THE SITE'S NORTH WING
The temple workshop
The building included Antoni Gaudí's studio, the artists' and artisans' studio and the store-room where the models, moulds and prototypes were created.

Alongside the apse. The workshop and the chaplain's residence took up the north chamfered corner of the block.

Anagram of the Sagrada Família
The symbol of Jesus, Mary and Joseph is on one of the workshop's walls.

The studio
The artists' work area had a roof with a skylight in it in order to provide as much sunlight as possible.

The furniture. Simple and functional, the workshop furniture is now on display in one of the school rooms.

A simple and functional building

When designing the schoolrooms, Gaudí looked for the utmost simplicity, using simple brick as the main material whilst devising a structure whose curved forms gave the arrangement a feeling of solidness or rigidity.

Wrought iron lamp
Despite the apparent simplicity of the basilica's schoolrooms, some of the decorative and functional details carried out were the result of great craftsmanship.